BENT, NOT BROKEN

JESSE VOGEL

First published 2015
Copyright © 2015 by Jesse Vogel
All rights reserved
ISBN: 978-1-56871-594-0

Published by

TARGUM PRESS
POB 27515
Jerusalem 91274
editor@targum.com

Distributed by
Ktav Publishers & Distributors Inc.

527 Empire Blvd.
Brooklyn, NY 11225-3121
Tel: 718-972-5449, 201-963-9524
Fax: 718-972-6307, 201-963-0102
www.Ktav.com

Printed in Israel

This book is dedicated to my Rebbe, Rabbi Avraham Leib Hershoff *zt'l*. He truly saved me in many ways when I was at a crucial crossroads in my life. His smile and hardy "boker tov" could light up a room, no matter how dark it was before. He and the Rebetzin practically adopted me, and later on my wife and children. They even have pictures of my family on their refrigerator. He was not only my Rebbe in Eretz Yisroel at Yeshiva Ohr Dovid for 2 years but he was my friend. Eight years later I was still speaking to him and Rebetzin Hershoff on a weekly basis, sometimes even more. We shared what was going on in each others lives, spoke to each other in learning, and his ear was always available when I needed advice. I truly miss our conversations more than I can express. His entire life was dedicated to others. He taught and inspired hundreds, if not thousands, of talmidim in Yeshivas Ohr David over more than 25 years, many of them having little to no previous exposure to Torah learning; and he worked for Torah Umesorah for more than 20 years. These are some of the things that he did publicly, he did untold other things privately. Everyone who came into contact with him is better for it. He is buried on Har Hazaysim where I am sure he was welcomed with open arms by his fellow tzadikim. The word is truly better for having had him in it and now it is noticeably more drab. I will forever miss my friend, my confidant, my Rebbe.

In honor of Moshe Dov Stein

Born in Caracas Venezuela and moved to America to learn in Yeshiva at 13

Rav of Far Rockaway Eruv and Shor Yoshuv Posek for over 25 years.

Always known for having an open home to all.

It is with joyful hearts that we celebrate the publishing of "Bent, Not Broken". Our children lived with us for the four months needed for their home to be renovated. It was a blessing to see our children and granddaughters daily! There were, of course,times when the reality of all they lost and the severe damage to their home caused anxiety....yet the result of the chesed and rebuilding was a home that was indeed safer and more beautiful. Hashem truly had a plan.

On a sad note, we must acknowledge the passing of Jesse›s Rebbi, Rabbi Avraham Leib Hershoff *ztl*, who guided Jesse in Yeshivah Ohr Dovid in Israel and beyond. He was a constant source of spiritual and practical guidance and friendship.We became close with him. Our friendship with his wonderful wife, Batya, continues. We miss him deeply.

For Julie and Jesse, and our granddaughters Devora Nechama, Basya and Miriam – May your home be a place of Shalom.

We love you! Mom and Dad, also known as Bubbe and Papa (Marilynne and Marty Vogel)

Alisa & I wish to dedicate this book to our three granddaughters,

Devora Nechama, Basya, and Miriam Vogel.

At the time of the hurricane, as young as they were, they exhibited courage and strength well beyond their years.

As much as their lives were disrupted, they carried on with an extremely mature understanding that belied their youth.

May Hashem continue to bless them and their parents for many more happy, healthy years.

Savta and Grandpa Alisa & Jeffrey Struzer

In Loving Memory of our parents

Eli and Sara Jedwab

אליעזר בן יעקב יצחק

ט״ז סיון תשנ״ט

May 31st 1999

שרה בת שמואל מרדכי הלוי

כ״ז אדר ב׳ תשנ״ז

April 4th 1997

Irving and Pearl Sommer

ישראל יהושע בן טוביה

ט״ו שבט תשל״ג

January 18th 1973

פערל בת ר׳ יצחק

כ׳ אלול תש״ג

September 10th 1990

May their memories be a blessing for us all

Dedicated by their children

Richard and Marilyn Jedwab
ירחמיאל ו׳מעטל אסתר יעדוואב

Grandchildren

Brian and Julie Jedwab

גדליה ו׳שמואלה יעדוואב

Ilana and Ilan Mandel

יהודית שפרה ו׳אילן זאב מאנדעל

And Great Grandchildren

Rebecca Lyndsey Jedwab

רבקה פערל יעדוואב

Amanda Lauren Jedwab

לייבע אסתר יעדוואב

Matthew Ian Jedwab

ישראל משה יעדוואב

Eliezer Yosef Mandel

אליעזר יוסף מאנדעל

Avraham Yitzchak Mandel

אברהם יצחק מאנדעל

Ayelet Fayga Mandel

אילת פייגא מאנדעל

Chana Avigayil Mandel

חנה אביגיל מאנדעל

Life …a beating heart, lungs contracting and expanding, nerves firing signals; in short, a miraculous occurrence. A miraculous occurrence which many of us take for granted as life can be snuffed out in a matter of seconds. We as a family have been worthy to survive what many people have not survived, the silent killer carbon monoxide poisoning. Sometimes we still lay awake at night replaying the whole ordeal and question why are we so worthy to still be here? Of course we will never know the true reason. However, we believe it is now our duty to spread the importance of carbon monoxide detectors and save lives.

We have heard of so many tragedies, heartbreaking, tear soaking tragedies in our times and at the same token we see such beautiful acts of chessed in our own community. May Hashem see all the good things that we do and may he spare us all from the poisons of this world.

With gratitude to Hashem for all that we have and all that we don't.

Yumi, Beth, Uriel Menachem, Gavriella & Orly

In honor of

Shira bas Yosef (Shirley Lewis Zimmerman) *Zt"zl*

Mikal ben Yaakov (Milton Zimmerman) *Zt"zl*

Rachel bas Tuvia (Rose Schlaffer Rodbell) *Zt"zl*

Eliezer ben Yosef Zvi (Leonard B. Rodbell) *Zt"zl*

By Pinchas and Tziryl Rodbell

L'iluy Nishmas

אברהם בן צבי

from Yoni & Yehudis Adlerstein

לע"נ ר' **אלעזר** בן **שלמה** הכהן

לע"נ ר' **דוד** בן **נתן נטע** הכהן

Dedicated in Loving Memory of our parents

Moshe Dov Ber   Sarah Rivka
Silverman

and

Menachem Ingber

and

Sabina and Julius Folman

Who were dedicated to their family and to Yiddishkeit,
to Tsedakah and to Chesed

By Tzvi and Bracha Ingber

In memory of

Mr. Philip Rubin

who would have told the victims of Hurricane Sandy "Don't give up the ship!".

It was his lifelong motto that gave hope to the hundreds-if not thousands, of the recipients of his Chesed. He was always there to lend a hand to those in need and would have been so proud of all the people whose acts of kindness are depicted in this book. May his memory be a blessing and his life an example to all of those whose lives he touched!

from the Katlowitz family

In honor of Jesse Vogel and his wonderful family

The courage that you have displayed throughout the last difficult eighteen months since Hurricane Sandy has truly been inspiring. Your dedication to your own family and of course your dedication to our community in keeping us safe is a real chizuk.

May you have continued success in all your endeavors and may all future projects and ideas only be for simchos and happy occasions.

All the best,

Rabbi Boruch Ber Bender and the entire Achiezer Team

In Honor of

the many wonderful Chesed organizations serving the Jewish community and with appreciation to our alumnus

Jesse Vogel

for sharing with us their selfless stories of salvation

Rabbi Lawrence and Nehama Teitelman

New Hyde Park, NY

In loving memory of our Grandparents

Rabbi Saadi ben Abraham

As a Great Rabbi of the Moroccan Community in Buenos Aires Argentina, during his 30 years of service, his wisdom and teachings transpired in the country's major Mass Media Communication as a Talmudic and Halachic scholar, a peace maker, and a devoted leader to his community and beyond.

Raquel bat Hachaham Hashalem Rebbi Yitzhak

An exemplary wife, a Tzadeket, a true Eshet Chayil, was the pilar of her husband's success, and an inspiration to the entire community. She only knew kindness. Her acts of chesed had no limits toward anyone who knocked their door, shul congregants, his talmidim, or even strangers

from the Benzaquen family

In memory of

Moshe ben Leib Ber Yaakov HaCohen

Beloved son, brother, husband, and father

He was always looking for opportunities
to do chesed for others.

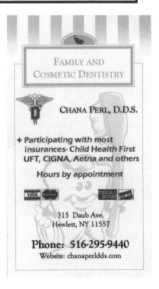

In loving memory of
Cynthia and Steven
Warshaw

from the Warshaw family

In memory of
Eliyahu Ben Mordechai
Goldwasser. A son,
husband, father, and
grandfather who loved to
give, and enjoyed seeing
others happy.

from the Goldwasser
family

In loving memory

of my parents

Walter & Esther Ducat ז״ל

Henry Ducat

I would like to express my gratitude to all of the families and businesses that donated money towards this book coming to fruition.

Mr. & Mrs. Wurtzel

Mr. & Mrs. Frischman

Mr. & Mrs. Lantor

Mr. & Dr. Golubovskaya

Rebetzin Kamenetzki

Mr. & Mrs Vogel

Phoenix Foods

Mr. & Mrs. Saidi

Mr. & Mrs. Goldwasser

Ms. Warshaw

Mr. & Mrs. Ducat

Mr. & Mrs. Salsberg

Ms. Hoch

Mr. & Mrs. Adlerstein

Dr. & Mrs. Rodbell

Mr. & Mrs. Kamel

Mr. Nathan

Mr. & Mrs. Katz

Mr. & Mrs. Langzum

Ms. Weiss

Ms. Frid

Mr. & Mrs. Hoffman

Mr. & Mrs. Singer

Mr. & Mrs. Danishrod

Mr. & Dr. Perl

Mr. & Mrs. Struzer

Mr. & Mrs. Mermelstein

Dr. & Mrs. Rosen

Mr. & Mrs. Rohani

Mr. & Mrs. Bornfreund

Mr. & Mrs. Rock

Mr. & Mrs. Benzaquen

Mr. & Mrs. Keller

Dr. & Mrs. Donath

Rabbi,Dr. & Rebetzin Ingber

Mr. & Mrs. Korman

Mr. & Mrs. Kashi

Mr. & Mrs Rodbell

Ms. Zuckerberg

Mr. & Mrs. Mittel

Mr. & Mrs. Weiner

Mr. Margolize

Mr. & Mrs. Sherman

Mr. & Mrs. Ickovic

Mr. & Mrs. Lev

Mr. & Mrs. Dinowitz

Dr. & Mrs. Kadar

Mr. & Mrs. Wexler

Mr. & Mrs. Simha

Mr. & Mrs. Brick

Mr. & Mrs. Herbst

Mittman Electrical Construction

Mr. & Mrs. Spurn

Mr. & Mrs. Jedwab

Alan's @ Brach's

Rabbi & Rebetzin Finman

Rabbi & Rebetzin Nathan

Coney Island Hospital minyan

Dr. & Mrs. Rapaport

Mr. & Mrs. Adler

RH Sibley Plumbing & Heating

Rabbi & Rebetzin Greenberg

Mr. & Mrs. Peretz

Mr. & Mrs. Gade

Rabbi & Rebetzin Messinger

The Jewish Home

Achiezer

Mr. & Mrs. Kohen

Ms. Genson

Mr. & Mrs. Hochizer

Rabbi & Mrs. Cooper

Mr. & Mrs. Murdakhayev

Dr. & Mrs. Glass

Exclusive Cabinetry & Design

Rabbi & Rebetzin Halpern

the Mold Master

Rabbi & Rebetzin Teitelman

Mr. & Mrs. Yagudaev

M. Weinraub Inc.

Mr. & Mrs. Monday

Mr. & Mrs. Rub

Mr. & Mrs. Unger

Judaica Plus

Rabbi & Rebetzin Bender

Abraham & Abraham Attorneys and Counselors at Law

FOREWORD

The story is told about a man who parked his new Bentley outside of a prestigious Midtown Manhattan bank and rushed in to see a bank official about a loan.

"I'd like to borrow $50,000 as soon as possible," he requested.

"Do you realize that in addition to your responsibility for the loan itself, you will be assuming the repayment of the interest at a high rate for the five years of the terms of this loan, should it be approved?" the clerk inquired.

"Yes! Absolutely!" the man responded.

"Now, do you have something you can use as collateral against the loan?" the bank clerk requested.

"Sure thing!" said the man. "That's my Bentley parked outside. Here are the keys. Take them!"

"Fine, here is your bank check for $50,000," said the clerk. He ordered the security guard to park the car in the bank's underground lot, and the man was on his way.

Just a week later, the man was back with the $50,000 cash plus the interest payment, to the bank clerk's utter surprise.

"If you had the money all along, why would you have bothered taking out the loan in the first place?" the clerk asked.

Handing over the $50,000 debt plus the twenty-five dollars in accumulated interest, the man responded, "Are you kidding? Where else can you get a week's underground parking in Midtown Manhattan for only twenty-five bucks?"

We have become a society of takers and manipulators. The better one maneuvers, the more he advances. Our approach to life has become one of "what's in it for me?" The days of "Ask not what your country can do for you; ask what you can do for your country," have been replaced with stimulus packages and bailouts. Our behavior is a far cry from that of Shmuel Hanavi, who absolutely refused to receive any benefit from anyone (see Berachos 10), or from the holy Tanna, Rabbi Pinchas Ben Yair, for whom Heaven intervened (see Chullin 7) to enable him to avoid benefiting from the hospitality of Rabbeinu Hakadosh. Although Chazal allow one the prerogative to derive pleasure from others, as Elisha Hanavi did in accepting the hospitality from the Ishah haShunamis, nonetheless there is no doubt that Elisha Hanavi did so only on the condition that he could reciprocate many times over (see the Meiri in Brachos 10).

The reason for this conduct of self-reliance was twofold: Firstly, so as not to become subservient to anyone but Hashem; secondly, so as not to develop the character trait of a "taker," irrespective of whether or not it was at someone else's expense. And although it would be unrealistic to equate ourselves with these great ba'alei madreigah, we would be terribly remiss if we allowed ourselves to succumb to the self-serving spirit of the "give me" generation. Unfortunately, this spirit has even penetrated some communities, where once politely requested and much appreciated financial support of parents and in-laws has now evolved into an expectation, if not a demand. It is a clear manifestation of the "tzu mir kumt" attitude which only reflects the "give me" posture of society at large.

My rebbi, Harav Shlomo Freifeld zt"l, would so passionately point out the greatness of the simple act of the previous generation to always respond to one's greeting of "A gut morgen (good morning)" with "A gut morgen, a gut yahr (good morning, good year)." Their motive was to ensure that they would always give back more than they received. You were kind enough to wish me a good day; I therefore wish you a good day, too, but in addition,

I also "give you" my blessing for a good year. (Of course this could go on forever!)

The story of Rav Preida (Eiruvin 54b) is an incredible demonstration of giving, and then giving even more. He had a student who had difficulty understanding the lesson. Rav Preida, one of the greatest Tanna'im of his day, took upon himself the responsibility to teach the lesson to this student until he'd finally "get it." Rav Preida proceeded to patiently review each lesson with him four hundred times until the student finally comprehended it. One time, in the course of teaching him, Rav Preida was interrupted with a message that he would be needed imminently for a mitzvah-related matter. He nonetheless continued to teach the lesson over and over again, until he had taught his student the requisite four hundred times. This time, though, the student still did not understand the lesson.

"Why is today different than other days?" Rav Preida asked his student.

The student answered, "Once the message came that the rebbi was needed for a mitzvah-related matter, I nervously anticipated that the rebbi might leave any minute, and I lost my concentration!"

Undaunted, Rav Preida said to his student, "Try to concentrate now, and I will teach it to you again." He then patiently taught him the material another four hundred times until the student understood. The Gemara concludes that Heaven rewarded Rav Preida for giving so much time to this student, and granted him four hundred more years to his life. When we give, not only do we not lose, but we gain the time and opportunities to give even more.

Indeed, in the introduction to Teshuvos Chasam Sofer, the Chasam Sofer writes that one should never think that helping out another Jew by learning with him will decrease his personal time for learning. Such thinking is built on the common distortion that we control our successes in Torah study, when in fact there is siyata d'Shmaya (Heavenly assistance) intimately involved (see Megillah 6). When one gives of his time, energy, and patience, and learns with others, the Ribono Shel Olam guarantees that the diminished amount of time that remains for his personal learning will be blessed with such clarity and lucidity, that it will enable him to stretch himself and accomplish more in less time.

Our tzaddikim's "giving" approach to life dates back to Avraham Avinu, who refused to take anything from the king of Sedom, and it has been their creed throughout the generations. In Kelm in the late 1800's, they would auction off various honors for the year on Simchas Torah. However, the bids were not for the honor of Chassan Torah or Chassan Bereishis, but for the honor to be the one to clean the beis medrash, or to kindle the heater, or to light the candles before davening. The honor of carrying the washing cup along with the heavy bucket of water, to enable the kohanim to have their hands washed before Birchas Kohanim, was bought by the Alter of Kelm himself. A young boy named Yerucham (later to become the famed Mirrer Mashgiach, Rav Yerucham Levovitz zt"l) once saw the Alter shlepping the bucket and wanted to relieve him, but the Rosh Yeshivah would not relinquish his hold on it. Clutching the bucket close to him, he said, "Young man! This is an honor I paid for. Please don't take it away from me!" Undoubtedly, such a role model made an indelible impression on this young boy destined to be mechanech the next generation.

The well-known story of Rav Moshe Feinstein zt"l and the car door is another example of this exemplary middah belonging to chashuve Yidden. A bachur who had given the Rosh Yeshivah a ride reached over to open the door for him and inadvertently slammed the door on Rav Moshe's finger. Although in great pain, Rav Moshe didn't utter a sound. The explanation was simple: This bachur was giving to me. I was taking from him. I should dare to make him feel bad for something he did unintentionally, while he was doing me a favor?!

It has been said in the sefarim hakedoshim that the very definitions of holiness and impurity are linked to whether one is a giver or a taker. Man's purpose on this world is to give, in order to reveal Hashem's name in the context of the personal world that he builds. Through that effort, he grows in holiness. The person who is absorbed in taking for himself will cave in to the negative middos of ga'avah, ta'avah, and the like and this will lead to a path of impurity and contamination.

When Rav Yochanan Hasandlar would make a shoe with the calculated intention that it be a strong shoe, a durable shoe, one that would serve its wearer well for many years, it was a "giving" act – and therefore an act of holiness. Compare such thinking with the "take as much as you can" attitude of todays "make to break and discard" manufacturers, and one understands that the impurity has spread way beyond the confines of promiscuity and licentiousness. The self-centeredness of the "taker" is sure to lead to the fragmentation that lies at the core of all that is impure. The greater the disintegration from the Source of all life, the greater the impurity will be.

On the other hand, the more we are "givers," the more we unite the creation, and the more we trace it all back to its one Source, the more progress we are making in a process of holiness. One could readily imagine the difference between marriages in which both parties are "takers" to one in which both parties focus on giving. In the home of the latter, there is not only peace and tranquility, but the Shechinah rests there as well, for the couple's giving nature has made their home a breeding ground for kedushah, allowing the Shechinah to feel comfortable there.

The blasphemy of the wicked Titus, the general of the Roman army who destroyed the second Beis Hamikdash, caused him to die with an unusual death. A Heavenly Voice rang out that the powerful Titus would be disgraced and destroyed by an insignificant "bri'ah kalah," a puny gnat, called disgraceful because it can only ingest but cannot expel. In the name of the Arizal, it is explained why that is so disgraceful: The gnat can only take in, but cannot give, therefore, it is removed from any semblance of holiness. Such is your lot, Titus!

Klal Yisrael is commanded: "Kedoshim tihiyu – You shall be holy." How much more so shall we, who are created in the image of Hashem, strive to be among the "givers," as we emulate our Creator and radiate holiness throughout the world.

During the events of Hurricane Sandy, Klal Yisroel once again showed their true colors with a display of giving that was beyond all expectations. There was a magnanimous outpouring for the unfortunate plight of the all too many victims of this catastrophe. Truckload after truckload, volunteer after volunteer, donation after donation: there was no end to the eternal giving of a nation that understands their role as sheluchei diRachmana – emissaries of Hashem.

My dear talmid, R' Yishai Vogel, who was intimately involved in the travesty of Sandy as a full-fledged victim has taken it upon himself to tell the story of so many as a personal expression of his *hakaras ha tov* and as an effort to bring to the forefront the valiant middah of a people who emulate Hashem's middah of chesed. "Viatah Michayeh es kulam – You, Hashem give life to all that exists." Just as You give life, so shall we.; and indeed the hundreds of volunteers and donors did exactly that as they literally infused life into those whose lives had been suddenly and abruptly interrupted.

In their merit and in the zechus of the great nachas ruach they undoubtedly brought to our Creator, may Hashem shower his brachos upon all of Klal Yisroel Ad bias goel Tzedek b'miheirah biyameinu amen.

Yehoshua Kurland

yud-gimmel Adar Rishon, 5774

THE QUIET BEFORE THE STORM

I can't believe that it has been more than 4 months since Hurricane Sandy. We have experienced so much *chesed* (help) that was orchestrated through *Siyata D'Shamaya* (divine providence). I had been planning on putting everything down on paper so that we would always remember this trying time, and how the *chesed* of others got our family through it. In a way it was going to be like a time capsule for future generations to look back on. I was just waiting for inspiration to strike to get started. In this context, I think "inspiration" was just a fancy way of saying procrastination.

We were recently at my sister's house for Pesach in Atlanta, and people kept asking us what we went through. Everyone I spoke to said that the *nisim* (miracles), both visible and hidden, and *Siyata D'Shmaya* (divine province), and *chesed* (help) that we experienced were so beautiful and awe inspiring that they really should be shared. Everyone told us that our experiences needed to find their way into the mainstream because they would inspire other people. I kept hearing different versions of that same response. It finally sank in, and I am starting now, *motzei* (after) Pesach 2013/5773.

If Hashem would have flooded our home and just kept us safe, dayeinu (it would have been enough).

I didn't think much about the hurricane when I first heard about it on the news, figuring that it would be the same overblown minor storm that Hurricane Irene had been. After all, the morning of the day the mayor decided to evacuate Far Rockaway and turn us into Sandy refugees was aesthetically beautiful.

Sunday, October 28th was sunny with a breeze. Before the mandatory evacuation was announced we had decided that because of the possible *sakana* (danger), Julie and the girls would not stay at the house with me. I thought that I would be able to handle more than they could, and in case things got very bad and I would have to flee it would be better if I was alone. I didn't want Julie and the girls to be in any danger, so, we made plans for them to go to her parents' house.

I went out to buy supplies like a generator, water, canned food, batteries, and the like — but Lowe's was out of generators. I remember slowly bending over and leaning on the shopping cart handles with my elbows, cradling my face in my hands, and feeling like a duck on a pond. To someone who was looking at me at that moment I appeared to be leaning on the shopping cart resting my head, but underneath my resting appearance my mind was moving a mile a minute, like the feet of a duck under the surface of the water fighting the current of the stream.

I remember going into internal crisis mode. It was as if a dam had burst in my head and my mind was flooded with thoughts and scenarios that were whirling around me. I felt like I was mentally drowning and trying to reach for a life raft. As soon as I had a thought or epiphany that could have helped us it slipped away. My thoughts and fears were coming fast and furious. What if I can't get a generator? Maybe Home Depot will have one. What if Home Depot runs out? Maybe a local hardware store? What if the local hardware stores run out? If the house gets flooded and I can't get a generator, maybe I can convert the power from my car's outlet to an extension cord and power the pump. What if there isn't enough power to power the pump? I was thinking of possible problems faster than I could grasp what I was thinking. I couldn't handle the turbulence swirling in my head any longer.

I started to sing the slow melody to *Esah Ainai* out loud. Right there in the middle of Lowe's. I didn't care who heard me. There was so much panic going on around me that I don't think anyone could hear me anyway, but at that point I didn't care either way. I was singing it in a low key and my voice kept cracking; I remember asking myself "why can't I keep my voice from cracking? The cracking is making me feel worse and more helpless, I'm falling apart; I need Julie".

I picked up my cell phone and called my wife. I was hoping that hearing her voice would be the reprieve that I so desperately needed to calm the storm in my head. I told her that they had no generators but I wasn't going to give up, I was going to keep looking for one. She said that she loved me and I said that I loved her and we hung up.

I then picked up my head from its cradle in my hands, took a deep breath and walked to the checkout line to pay. While waiting online I heard an announcement over the PA system. The sales associate on the loudspeaker said that they were about to receive a large shipment of generators. At first I thought that I was hearing things, but *Baruch Hashem* my suspicions were confirmed that I heard correctly because I saw droves of people running to the back of the store to wait on line for those precious generators to be unloaded. I quickly paid for my items and drove home as fast as I could, since my trunk was full and a generator is large and too heavy to put on the roof rack. I unpacked the car in the driveway and asked Julie and the kids to put the things away while I ran back to the store to get one of those priceless generators.

Baruch Hashem I got one of the last ones. They cost about $750, but it was well worth it because that $750 wasn't just purchasing a generator. It was buying hopes and dreams. At that moment, those hopes were hopes of being able to help my family and keep my house safe and dry. Those dreams were dreams of self-sufficiency, knowing that if the worst case scenario should happen, I would be able to provide my own power and be able to help others in need. That there would be a day after tomorrow and a day after that and a day after that.

There were some people buying multiple generators; I assumed that they were buying them for friends and relatives who couldn't get to the store at a moment's notice. I remember thinking to myself that that was an incredibly nice thing to do, to overextend yourself financially to help a loved one.

The lines were so long that they wrapped around the entire store. I have never seen such long lines in my entire life. You could feel the tension and fear in the air. People were excited to be able to get a generator but uneasy because they were out of gas cans to fill them with fuel. When I looked around I noticed that everyone was constantly either tapping their foot on the floor or religiously checking their watches and or cell phones at least once a minute. I also noticed a sense of camaraderie. People were talking to perfect strangers about their fears and hopes. People were asking each other if anyone knew how to use a generator and or if anyone knows what else they could do to protect their homes and possessions. People were leaving their shopping carts in their spots in line and walking up and down the line to ask other people all sorts of questions. I even saw some people helping others by drawing diagrams of what they should do when they get home on the outsides of the boxes of the generators. They were also exchanging phone numbers so they could call and ask questions and be walked through the steps needed to take when they got home. It was really a beautiful thing to see how everyone was coming together to help perfect strangers in their time of need.

Unfortunately the positive environment seemed to end at the door to the store. When I got to the parking lot I was very disappointed in how their *yetzer haras* (evil inclination) had taken advantage of some of them. Some people were waiting for the store to run out of generators and turning around and selling them in the store's parking lot for $1,700 cash. I felt like some of the human spirit had died at that moment. It's hard to fathom what kind of blackened soul a person must have to take advantage of people when they are at their most vulnerable and desperate state.

Buying a gas can was much more difficult than you would expect. There were none to buy anywhere, not 5 gallons or 5 ounces. Apparently I was the last one to take this storm seriously. I and many other people were scrambling to find gas cans. After all, what good is a gas powered generator without gasoline?

That Sunday morning before the hurricane hit I remembered that my parents had a ½ gallon gas can for their snow blower and that they were far enough from the coast that they wouldn't need it. The generator that I purchased required 7 gallon at a time, but I was excited to realize that I could get that ½ gallon gas can because it was more than I had. While I was driving to my parents' house to borrow the gas can, I decided to call my mother and tell her my predicament and ask if I could borrow the gas can.

On my way there I saw a closed automotive supply store with several 5 gallon gas cans in its window that practically had rays of sunshine being emitted by them. I quickly downshifted into second gear, hit 5,000 RPM and evaded other cars on the road as I slid into the first spot in the parking lot in front of the stores entrance with dramatic flair. It was as if all the drivers on the road had all simultaneously spotted them at the same time as I had and it was a race to see who could get there first. I abruptly ended the phone call with my mother and got out of my car feeling like I had won the lottery. It was as if the clouds had parted to let the sun shine directly upon me. I was so elated that for a moment I had forgotten all about the hurricane that I was so worried about making an appearance at my doorstep. It was 8:47 AM and the sign on the stores window said that it would open at 9AM.

Knowing that there were no other stores in the area that had any gas cans in their inventory I was surprised that I was the only one so far to realize that this was the place to be. I stood outside that door until they opened and I bought all six of their 5 gallon gas cans. I only wanted 3 for myself but I had made a pact with one of my neighbors, who was also not able to locate any gas cans. We agreed that if either of us were able to locate some, we would buy for the other, so 3 were for him. By the time I put the last one in my car I heard people walking out of the store, happy to be able to buy 1 gallon gas cans.

I quickly went to the gas station and filled up my car and my three gas cans. Then I returned to my house; I felt like a conquering hero who had braved the wilds of Far Rockaway and the Five Towns and returned victorious with my 15 gallons of stored gasoline. When I went to take them out of my trunk, I covered them with garbage bags to make sure that some of the unsavory people on my block didn't see them so they wouldn't be stolen. They seemed to be more precious than gold. Little did I know how true that would become in the days and weeks to come.

Later that morning, my oldest daughter, Devora Nechama, had a birthday party to go to in Bayswater for one of her friends from her class in TAG (Torah Academy for Girls). We took her to the birthday party and as she got out of the car we told her to have a great time and that we would pick her up later.

As soon as she shut her door we turned the radio on to the news. We were listening to them talk about the need for the mayor to make a decision about whether or not to declare evacuations because it takes a lot of time and work to evacuate the areas in consideration. We hung on every word. We breathed a sigh of relief when there were no orders for mandatory evacuation.

We turned on an Uncle Moishy CD for the girls and drove home. When we got home Julie reminded me to affix some wood to the windows like I had done for Hurricane Irene. I said that we didn't need it. I was summarily overruled by Julie and reminded of what had happened during Hurricane Irene. During Hurricane Irene, I had cut pieces of 2x4 and drilled holes in them and fastened them to the stucco around the windows. Each window had 2 pieces of 2x4 attached on an angle in order to cover more surface area to protect the windows from flying debris and from falling branches from the tree next to the house.

*The windows being protected by wood in
preparation for Hurricane Irene*

During Hurricane Irene two branches broke free from the tree from the gale force winds and were hurled toward our house. Through unbelievable *Siyata d'Shmaya* one hit the middle of the piece of wood protecting a dining room window and the other hit the middle of the piece of wood that was protecting a living room window. The only reason that I was aware of this *nes* (miracle) was because when I went to check on the house afterward I found big branches on the ground lying up against the house underneath each of the aforementioned windows and upon closer inspection I found deep gashes taken out of those 2 pieces of wood. I was less than enthusiastic about it, but she was right, and I got the ladder and reattached the pieces of wood to the house to protect the windows again.

We had heard about a family event at Lowe's called Build and Grow that was scheduled to start right after the birthday party ended. It sounded like a nice thing to do for both us and the kids so we decided to go.

We kept listening to the radio to see if the mayor was going to order the evacuation of Far Rockaway. He did. We couldn't believe our ears; we had heard the very words that we had hoped to never hear. THE ORDER WAS MADE FOR THE MANDATORY EVACUATION OF FAR ROCKAWAY! We paused to process the news. My wife and I looked at each other and told each other that it would be OK. We decided to let Devora stay at the birthday party and to even go to the Build and Grow event at Lowe's before we evacuated to break the tension and try to not scare the children too much.

When we picked up Devora, we told the parents that were there about the evacuation. They each reacted the same way. They paused and looked at us with a puzzled look and replied "really?", "Are you sure?" We told them that unfortunately we were sure.

We went straight to Lowe's from the party. While walking through Lowe's we heard people talking about the storm. The hurricane seemed to be all that anyone could think about or talk about. The somber mood changed when we got to the area where we would be building the projects. There was only one other family there to participate in the family event with us, our friends the Winzelburgs, who were the ones who told me about the event in the first place.

We had a fantastic time at Lowe's. It was almost like we were enveloped in a wonderful mirage of tools and balsa wood where the impending storm couldn't find us. Our kids were so excited. They each received their own Lowe's apron with their name on it, work goggles, a cute little child size hammer and screwdriver, and an unassembled project. We had a lot of fun. After about an hour, each child had completed building their own little box for keepsakes and decorated it in their own special way.

When it was time to leave our friends told us that they were going straight from Lowe's to his parents' house in Staten Island to be safe. Little did he know the level of the storm's fury that was going to be unleashed on Staten Island as well, but *Baruch Hashem*, they were going to be staying in a safe area.

At that point I kept hearing news broadcasts about the impending storm. They kept reiterating that it would not be a miniscule occurrence like Hurricane Irene. I started to regret my decision to stay home and protect the house from looters as well as being there to continue to refill the gas powered generator to maintain the electric supply for our refrigerator as well as our sump pump in the basement. I began to be aware that every time I would hear a news briefing about how this hurricane was not going to just lie down and play dead like the previous one, my stomach would get tied in knots. I finally realized that my stomach had more *saychel* (common sense) than I did.

Interestingly enough, throughout my brief period of insanity of assuming I would be able to stay home during the storm, my mother would call every once in a while and ask if I was still sure about my decision. I kept replying that I would stay home because it was probably being overblown just like Hurricane Irene. About five minutes after I had my epiphany that staying home was beyond foolish, we received a phone call from the *Rebbetzin* (wife of the Rabbi) of the *Rav* (Rabbi) who is responsible for being *mekarev* (reintroduced us to our Judaism) both my wife and myself. Just a little bit of background that is important when it comes to understanding the conversation that we had with her. Her daughter had just finished being treated for cancer with chemotherapy and radiation. That conversation over the phone went as follows: She said that parents with sick children are willing to pump their children with poison in order to make them healthy again...you are deciding to do something stupid that could not only kill you but make your children orphans... This conversation went on for several minutes, after which I replied that we had made the decision to leave the house.

During that phone call we realized that my mother had orchestrated the phone call by contacting someone that she knew we would respect and hopefully listen to. At that point I made a deal with my wife. I said that if we went to my parents' house I would feel more comfortable because we would have more room than at my in-laws. Also, they have a cat that I am allergic to, and my mother was home alone since my father with in China on a business trip. After some serious deliberation the decision was made that we would go to my parents' house to weather the storm.

We started to remove our valuables from the basement and place them on the first floor where we had assumed they would be safe because our first floor is between 5 and 6 feet above ground level.

We removed things from the basement, like my tools, important keepsakes, paper goods that would be ruined in the basement if it flooded, and we loaded up our cars with picture albums, our laptop, our back-up hard drive, the silver from the breakfront, jewelry, enough clothing for a few days, some food, bottled water, my tefillin (phylacteries), some *seforim* (Jewish books) so I could continue learning daf yomi (a daily Talmud learning schedule), a few tools that might come in handy, and of course my guns and ammunition. I even removed the car seats from the back seats of my car and folded them down flat in order to be able to carry more things in my car.

After we finished loading our cars with all of our important possessions we went into the living room. As a cohesive unit, our family joined hands to make a circle the middle of the living room. I started to address my family. I remember saying "look at the people whose hands we're holding in this circle. This is our family. We are each other's most prized and important possessions. Everything that we're standing in and that you see when you look around us are just things. Everything can be replaced except for the members of this family. As nice as our home, toys, and clothing are, they can all be replaced" and I remember repeating that "they can all be replaced, we cannot. We are all that is important and we are making this decision as a family for the good of our family. We are going to leave our house not knowing what we're going to come back to. Whether we lose all of our things or we come home to see that nothing happened, as long as we are together we will be fine".

At that point I looked over to my wife and saw that she was crying and I remember saying to her that "this wonderful family of ours cannot be replaced at any cost and we are what's most important and everything else can be replaced they are just things and it will be alright". At that point I remember getting choked up myself and looking at the faces of my beautiful family and seeing that they were looking around at everything that was surrounding us.

Our oldest daughter, Devora Nechama said that "it will be alright as long as we have each other, it will be okay". That simple sentence being uttered by my daughter was one of the proudest moments of my life, and unbeknownst to me, in the coming months, that single sentence brought me more strength and courage that I think I could have mustered on my own. We kept reiterating that Hashem has a plan for us and he will make sure that we are safe and protected.

At that point my older two daughters, my wife, and I each in our own words said goodbye to the house and asked Hashem to keep us and our home safe. As we walked out the door, we made sure to kiss the mezuzah one by one. I remember as I locked the door feeling a rush of emotions as the dead bolt clicked into the locked position. I felt fear, anxiety, anger, depression, defeat, and in the back of my mind I dared to feel a sliver of hope. Hope that our prayers would be answered with a favorable outcome. We got in our cars and began to drive away from a *makom sakkana* (a place of danger) toward what we hoped would be a safe place.

EVACUATION

I drove my possession-laden car while my wife drove her minivan filled with the children and a trunk full of our things. We decided to take both cars with us because, if the news was correct about the strength and devastation that was to come, we thought it would be thoughtless and irresponsible to leave one car to be destroyed and only have one car at our disposal. We set off on our journey in tandem, with my wife taking the lead in our own little convoy to safety. We headed down the Nassau Expressway to find that all of the side streets had been closed off by barricades and the police, and the traffic lights had been disabled to speed up the traffic on the 878, where during normal hours, heavy traffic was tedious at best. I can honestly say it was the most ominous drive of my life.

I felt like an extra from an Armageddon movie or from a reenactment of a story that you would hear about a city that was preparing to be invaded or bombed. We were only a few blocks from our house and I already felt like a downtrodden refugee. Everywhere you looked, as far as you could see, there was an ocean of metal. People just like us trying to get out of harm's way, to find safety in a location where we didn't even know if we would be safe. People were so involved in their own fears that they didn't even cut other people off; they just followed each other's lead as if they were a part of a train heading to wherever the collective destinations were. Throughout the entire drive of our convoy to my parents' house, my wife and I were on the phone with each other and talking about how we couldn't believe what we were seeing, what we were a part of, and worried about the uncertain future of our home, neighbors, friends, and neighborhood.

The evacuation route on the Nassau Expressway near Burnside Ave
with Julie and the kids in the blue minivan in front of me

When we eventually pulled up to my parent's house my mother, Bubbs (short for *Bubbe*) was there waiting for us. She thanked us for making the smarter harder decision. I thanked her for allowing us to live in her house but I didn't show her the level of *hakaras ha tov* (gratitude) that she deserved. I thought that we were only going to need to stay there for a few days and then move back home and pick up the pieces.

My family went inside and I started to unload the car in a slow, melancholy, and wearisome fashion. It seemed to be a daunting and never-ending task. The whole time I was removing our belongings from the two cars I found myself humming *ani ma'amin* (I believe) to a slow and morose tune, stopping occasionally to wipe the tears from my eyes and choke back the feeling coming from the back of my throat that kept me from completely breaking down. I kept telling myself I had to at least appear strong to try to keep the family together and in the most positive spirits we could muster. I had to stop and take a break several times in order to stave off reaching the point of breakdown where I would not be useful.

I think that one of the hardest parts of this entire ordeal was hiding my inner fear and trying to maintain a positive facade for the sake of my wife and children. It was up to me, the head of the household, to make my wife and children feel safe even when my *emuna* (belief) had been shaken and I was running on fumes.

Up until this point I was only able to hear what other people told me about the hurricane and what I heard on 1010 WINS because we don't have a television in our house. At my parents' house I was able to watch the news on their television, which was truly frightening because I was able to see the damage the hurricane had already done and the havoc it was already wreaking while on the course towards my home.

We brought the children's things upstairs to the room that all three of them were going to be sharing and my wife and my things to the basement where we were going to be staying. I found myself sitting at the edge of the bed staring at the blank television screen just whispering *tefillos* (prayers) to Hashem (G-D), begging and pleading for our safety and the strength to endure.

At that point when I felt I had reached rock bottom, my wife, Julie, came downstairs and sat next to me, as if she knew I needed the strength of her presence there with me. She was and continues to be my kindred spirit. After just sitting there without saying a word for a few minutes Julie said some of the most important and powerful words that I could have heard at that moment. She said "it is going to be okay". She said it partially for me to gain strength and partially for her to hear it said aloud and gain strength from it as well. She said it was time to go upstairs.

We both got up and walked upstairs together. I'm not sure exactly how long I was sitting on the edge of that bed in the basement by myself thinking, but it seems like an eternity and I'm not sure how long I would've remained down there if my kindred spirit had not come to claim me from the abyss of my thoughts. She was able to walk up the stairs and out of the basement door to be with the family, while I needed to pause at the top of the stairs, take a deep breath and let out an audible sigh. I continued walking to rejoin the family with a smile that was hollow and only skin deep and it was all that I could do to avoid letting my inner turmoil be visible to the children.

I was able to snap out of my melancholy mood when we were sitting at the dining room table. There were even jokes told at the table, which felt comforting. While at the table it felt like someone had changed our channel. We even had a lighthearted conversation during dinner after which we put the girls to bed and told them the same important words Julie told me that brought me so much strength and comfort. Everything is going to be okay.

After the kids were asleep we went to the room with a television to see what was going on. To see how our fears were playing out. Hearing the news anchors' impossible scenarios and expectations for damage was truly heart-wrenching. Then I couldn't believe what I was seeing. People living in the Rockaways, who were in the greatest danger, were planning to stay and ride out the storm. They were showing videos of these people, whose backyards were literally on the beach, playing with their kids. Their kids were climbing the man-made jetties that were put there to protect them from the tidal surge. The amount of senselessness and the level of irresponsibility of these people were unfathomable. I remember not understanding how someone could put their children in harm's way like that and I wondered why they weren't being arrested for child endangerment or at least being issued summonses for blatant stupidity. They had no regard for their own lives and the lives of their children, or for the first responders who were willing to put themselves into a *makom sakkana* to go out there and rescue them from their own ridiculousness.

On that note, we decided to go downstairs. Even after we went downstairs, to sleep in the bedroom that my parents had supplied for us, which was warm and comfortable in their basement, I was unable to sleep. It was probably the most frightening and endless night of my life. I could not fall asleep; all I did was watch the news. Going from channel to channel, hearing the same thing while hoping that the next reporter was going to say that it was a mistake or that the hurricane made a turn and it was going out to sea. I think at that point my eyes were the only part of me that was functioning and I wasn't taking in any information. My mind was so oversaturated that nothing could penetrate. I was just struck with an intense paralyzing and penetrating fear to the point of numbness.

Eventually I fell asleep, for probably only an hour or two, and woke to quickly scramble for the remote control to turn on the television in hopes of hearing the broadcast that I had hoped to hear all night. Unfortunately, I didn't get the news that I was yearning for. In fact, the storm had made a turn in our direction and it had slowed it's already stammered pace. The reporters said that we were in for a prolonged punishing event and that people should not venture outside once it starts unless it is absolutely necessary.

As the day wore on we started to get a small taste of the storm. The wind picked up and the skies began to darken. I remember feeling anxious and restless because I had an inkling about what was about to happen, but I was powerless to do anything about it. Nothing had really happened yet and I already felt like a helpless victim. I noticed that my Bubbs and Papas' dog, Charlie, a 70 pound giant schnauzer was becoming restless and their bird, Boe, a Myer parrot, made more noise than usual. This trend increased as Sandy drew closer.

I was so anxious that I couldn't keep still. I felt like an animal pacing from one end of my cage to the other. I was fighting my urges to get back to my house to see how it was doing and make sure that it was safe and protected. I know it would be a fool's errand, but in that kind of situation I wasn't thinking clearly. I had too many emotions and thoughts going through my head. Luckily I had Bubbs and Julie there to practically take my car keys so I wouldn't go. Instead of using force, they used logic and guilt. We were so glued to the television that watching the news was practically a drug that we were addicted to. When I would take a break from watching the news and spend time with the children, go to the bathroom, wash dishes, or go to daven (pray) at shul (synagogue) I would yearn for the news and it would be on my mind like I was an addict going through withdrawal.

We went into the backyard looking for things that with enough wind could become projectiles. We put toys, tables, and chairs in the garage or house to preempt any possible loss of property or dangerous situations and we hunkered down as if we were in a bomb shelter waiting for the all clear. The more we watched the more scared we became. They just went on and on about the worst case scenarios and the level of devastation that we should expect and telling us that life in New York City wouldn't get back to normal for quite some time. I remember going out to daven and constantly looking out of my sunroof when I would go near a tree, looking for falling trees and branches. The wind began to howl through the trees and make them sway. I looked at every tree as if it was a lurking assassin waiting for me to not pay attention and it would strike and pounce on unsuspecting victims. Everywhere I went, all I saw were things that could be thrown at my car as debit. Garbage cans, downed branches, toys, lawn gnomes, street signs, mailboxes; in my eyes, they might as well have been scud missiles aimed at me. I was wary of everything and anything. When I would be inside my parents' house I kept looking at their neighbors' tree across the street. A towering Oak that was past its prime, just taunting my fears and anxieties. Every time its branches would move from the robust wind gusts I was sure that it was beckoning me to dare to come outside so it could crush my car.

Before the wind and rain reached critical mass we decided to pull all four cars into my parents' driveway where they would be safe, like four small huddling children hiding behind the house finding strength in numbers and proximity. All I cared about was that they would be as far away from that beckoning tree across the street as possible. From then on, we stayed inside except to walk the dog either in the yard or a few houses down making sure to stay away from trees and power lines just in case the winds became too much for them and they would come crashing down upon us *chas v'shalom* (G-D forbid), or to go to shul.

Bubbs and Julie soaking wet after walking the dog

Baruch Hashem that never happened and *Hakodosh Baruch Hu* (G-D) kept us all safe, for which I am and always will be eternally grateful.

DURING THE STORM

During the height of the storm, it was necessary for us to find ways to occupy both our time and our minds, which was not an easy task. We played games with the children, read books, I learned *daf yomi*; we did anything we could think of to keep busy. We constantly had the feeling that we were going to *chas v'shalom* lose power at any moment. I was as prepared as possible for as many situations as I could think of. I had guns and ammunition just in case people lost their minds to the point that they would start to loot. I had chainsaws, an ax and 2 hatchets just in case a tree would come down and need to be broken up. I had a 10,000lb tow rope/chain just in case those pieces of tree/debris would need to be moved out of the street or a car or other large piece of debris needed to be relocated. I had flashlights and batteries and an emergency radio. I had a cooler with ice in it and 4 five gallon bottles of water. I even brought a few new buckets just in case the sewers would back up and we needed to use them as toilets.

Baruch Hashem most of them were not needed for their intended purposes. With *Hakodosh Baruch Hu's* (G-D's) help we never lost power, cell phone reception, internet access, or television service. We were able to watch the news and the kids were able to watch shows about animals and Uncle Moishey videos. Everyone was as happy and comfortable as you could be during a hurricane. When I would look out the windows and see the trees swaying and the street signs moving so much that they were starting to pull their poles out of the ground, I became nervous yet hopeful. Was this all there was going to be? Just some shaking signs, trees swaying in the gusty wind, and rain. I thought to myself, this isn't so bad. We can handle this. It's just a lot of wind and rain. The streets weren't even flooded.

I vividly remember what happened next. The kids went to sleep and the news was turned on. I remember being there with Julie and I was paralyzed and slack jawed as a result of what I was looking at. I didn't even realize that I was still standing in front of the couch holding the remote instead of sitting like I had intended. I was watching video of lower Manhattan under water with boats in the streets. I couldn't believe my eyes. I felt a very unpleasant shiver go up my spine. I had forgotten that the place where I was had not been hit as hard as the place I had come from. Then I watched the Battery Tunnel have a veritable river flow into it, and then, as if I hadn't had enough, they showed the Rockaways. Not exactly where I live, but a place I recognized. It was only a 5 minute drive from my house that I passed every day on my way to and from work. There was at least 8 feet of water on the streets and they were rescuing people from their homes from the second floor because the first floors were completely submerged. I couldn't believe what I was seeing. Was this a bad dream or a nightmare? I couldn't take it anymore. My mind was overwhelmed with anxiety, fear, and a bad case of the "what ifs". What if we lose power? What if the basement floods? What if our house gets completely destroyed? What if we lose everything? The what ifs came fast and furious. I needed to find a way to make them stop. Julie and I turned off the TV and told each other that it was going to be alright. We said that if the worst should happen and we lose everything, we will rebuild and be stronger than ever. Saying it was easier than doing it but hearing it was what was important at that moment.

My wife and I both poured each other potent nightcaps and decided to call it a night. The thoughts that were going through our heads were more than we could bear. We headed downstairs to our temporary home away from home and both plopped ourselves down on the beds with noticeable sighs, as if sighing out loud would help make all of our problems go away. We told each other that we loved each other very much and then we recited our new mantra as if we were our own Hurricane Sandy support group, "it will all be ok, we will get through this as a team, and we are not doing this alone". At times it felt as if I was alone. Not because my wife and parents weren't overly supportive, but because I had a "head of the household during a crisis" syndrome. One of my problems is that I over think things and think of possible scenarios, what-ifs and just-in-cases. I felt alone sometimes because I spent too much time inside my own head worrying and not expressing myself as much as I should to my familial support group. I had a bad case of the "duck on the pond" syndrome. True, all I was doing was lying in bed but I couldn't stop the gears in my head from spinning a mile a minute. Luckily, my pre-sleep l'chaim began to work and I started to drift off to sleep.

When I woke up at about 5 AM, I couldn't see what was going on outside because we were sleeping in the basement and there were only 2 small windows. Each had a frosted coating on it and they were only about 4 inches high and about 10 inched wide. Just because I couldn't see what was going on outside didn't mean that I didn't have an idea of what was going on. I could hear the howling of the wind outside and the sound of garbage cans flying around the street hitting cars and houses. Luckily I was still tired from my nerves and my nightcap. I decided to shut out the world for a little bit longer, so I closed my eyes and went back to sleep. I was abruptly woken up by my daughter jumping on me and saying something emphatically but I was half asleep and what she was saying didn't process well. I remember grabbing her shoulders gently to get her to stop jumping and pulled her close and whispered "good morning D (short for Devora Nechama), why are you here"? She said that I "have to come upstairs, it's crazy outside." She was so excited; I didn't know she could speak so fast. She was telling me about the trees bending and the branches and leaves flying around and the street signs moving. So I slowly sat up and started to walk to the bathroom to wash nagel vasser (the morning ritual washing of the hands). I was so tired I was dragging my feet. I am not sure where my lethargic state was coming from. Was it coming from just being woken up suddenly from a deep sleep? Was it coming from being emotionally drained? I am not quite sure, but it didn't matter. My daughter was scared and excited at the same time and needed me to go upstairs to keep her company. So I did what any parent would do. I found that parental energy source and threw on my clothing and started my day.

Once I made it upstairs I was overwhelmed with how cute my daughters were. All three of my daughters were awake and engaged in activities already. Miriam, my youngest, who was 2 ½ years old, was very busy "reading" a book while sitting on the couch. Basya, who was 4 ½ years old, was lying on the ground next to the farmhouse toy making the animals have a conversation in a voice that was so high pitched that only the dog really knew what she was saying, and Devora Nechama, who was 7 years old, was standing on the toy piano by the front window beckoning for me to come join her while she was surveying what was going on outside.

She was so enthusiastic about everything she saw. At one point she saw what looked like an urban tumbleweed made out of what appeared to be someone's uprooted bush rolling down the street being propelled by a huge gust of wind. She leapt into my arms and clung to me like a spider monkey and emphatically said "Tatti (Dad), Tatti, did you see that? That bush is so scared of the hurricane that it is running away!" At which point we locked eyes, looked at each other as a smirk began to show itself at the corner of her mouth and slowly spread to the rest of her face when we exploded in a loud burst of laughter. I threw her on my back and started to run around the house yelling that we should run away from the hurricane and find a good place to hide from the storm. It was a beautiful thing. She was belly laughing and making suggestions as to where I should run to next. "Tatti, make a right, head into the kitchen", "make a left and hide in the bathroom", "quickly, let's hide in the coat closet". We had a lot of fun pretending that we could hide from the hurricane.

While we were playing our game of "hide from the hurricane" I had a fleeting thought. I remember thinking to myself "*Baruch Hashem* we went to my parents' house where we are safe, dry, and have electricity and heat", and I started to think about the hardships and fear that people were going through that either didn't have a safe place to go or who decided to stay and ride out the storm. They weren't having fun like this playing "hide from the storm"; they were living it with real fear in their hearts, not pretending to be scared. I also started to think about those poor idiots that I had seen on the news that lived in houses that were right on the water in the Rockaways that were going to stay and ride out the storm with their little kids. I wondered what they were going through at that moment. Then I snapped out of it and was back to playing with my kids. While we were running around the house I noticed that we weren't alone, we were being followed. My other 2 daughters were in hot pursuit. The youngest one was holding a banana while she ran, so the dog was following her as the caboose while trying to sneak in banana flavored licks. It was quite cute to watch. He really wanted that banana but was being careful to not knock her over taking it. Even though he weighs more than 3 times what she does when fully clothed and sopping wet, he wouldn't take it from her. He just happily followed her while wagging his tail, patiently waiting for her to drop it.

Eventually the dog let us know that he had to go outside for a walk. I put on my rain boots and raincoat and put him on his leash and took him out the back door of the house to the part of the street farthest from big trees. He didn't make it very far, probably less than 50 feet from the house before he did his business and pulled me back to the house. The entire minute or so that I spent walking him was spent looking up at power lines and trees looking for any signs of danger. I was not in the mood to get flattened by a tree or electrocuted by a downed power line. That minuscule excursion to the outside was enough that I was soaked everywhere that wasn't covered by my coat. I went downstairs to change my drenched socks and pants and take off my shoes to dry.

At that point I decided it was time to wake up Julie. We then turned on the news and got our first glimpse of good news. It said that the hurricane was almost at its peak for our area and that it would soon start to move away and that we would *im yirtza Hashem* (with G-Ds help) start to see Sandy's fury decrease soon. We were elated. Our spirits were finally doing their preflight checks and ready to soar. The next thing I heard on the news was that Coney Island Hospital was being evacuated because of the power outages and flooding. I was worried for my patients' safety. I am an Occupational Therapist there. I treat outpatients and inpatients as well as evaluate inpatients' functional status and evaluate their equipment needs for when they go home to make sure that they have what they need so as not to reinjure themselves and be safe in their home environment. As worried as I was, I wasn't going to work until at least Wednesday. I decided that my family's wellbeing and safety was more important to me than my patients, especially when I saw that they had a lot of local staff and volunteers assisting in the evacuation process. Even if I wanted to go to work, my wife and mother wouldn't have allowed it. They would have taken my keys while I slept and hidden them if they had to. The only place I was allowed to go during the hurricane was to shul for davening and to walk the dog.

AFTER THE STORM

Finally, *Baruch Hashem* (thank G-D), *nisim v'niflaos* (miracles and wonders), the storm started to wane. The torrential downpours became a drizzle, the wind went from gale force to a breeze, the clouds began to thin out and the sunshine was trying to show its wonderful face that we had missed. We felt like flowers during the winter, longing for the sunshine. We began to feel our leaves growing and the color of our petals begin to regain their robust and youthful hue. Towards the end of the day we really started to feel more and more rejuvenated.

It was Tuesday morning, the sun was shining and the birds were chirping and everything seemed to be right with the world. I was even able to see an entire rainbow when I looked out of my parents' front window. It was as if Hashem was saying that the *mabul* (flood) was over and that today was a new day and that our troubles were behind us.

A friend of mine, Yudie Gross, had stayed behind and endured the storm. He went driving once most of the waters had receded, and sent me a picture of my daughters' school, T.A.G. elementary school. It's first floor had been flooded and ruined.

I knew that another one of my friends, Simon Springer, had also stayed behind because he had to work at a local store. He lived far enough away from the beach that he didn't get affected from the flood waters. He just had to deal with the blackouts. He ventured to my house but was unable to get there because my block is a dead end and I am the last house on the right and the street goes slightly downhill in the direction of my house. There was too much water for him to be able to get all the way to my house with his Toyota SUV. He got as close as he could and texted me this picture:

Torah Academy for Girls elementary school after most of the flood waters had subsided

The light beige house on the right was our house with cars and toys that had floated away from their positions from before the flood waters

I was hoping to go to our house that morning, but after seeing his picture and what he texted me I decided to go a little bit later in the day. I wouldn't have been able to get to the house that morning unless I had a boat. My wife and mother tried very hard to talk me out of it and to wait one more day.

I couldn't handle waiting one more day to see what had happened with my own eyes. I needed to go, and I needed to go now.

THE TRIP TO THE HOUSE

I started to think about what problems I might encounter on my way. I decided to take an ax, two hatchets, a battery-operated power drill and chain saw, my 10,000 Lb tow rope/chain, water proof boots, a good flashlight, a gun and some ammunition. That way I could cut up and remove anything in my way, see what happened in our basement because we had no windows in the basement, and defend or rid the house of looters if need be. The local streets were littered with debris. I saw huge downed trees, some even crushing cars and leaning on houses, garbage cans strewn about, and lawn furniture and lawn decorations everywhere.

Bubbs standing next to a huge fallen tree that Baruch Hashem fell away from the house that it is in front of

I decided to use the highway in the hope that it wasn't closed due to flooding or a downed tree blocking the road. Luckily, the local highways were open with minimal debris on the road, mostly small twigs and leaves. It was smooth sailing until I hit Brookville Boulevard near the wetlands.

Brookville Boulevard is a narrow winding road that cuts through the wetlands and often floods when it rain. I had assumed that I wouldn't get through but decided to try because it was normally the quickest route to get to my house. I noticed that cars kept turning around but didn't know why. I had assumed that it was because it was flooded. I was wrong. They were turning around because the flood waters had subsided and left a 30-foot boat sitting in the middle of the road. It was impassable. I took my phone out to take a picture but when I was just about ready to take the picture, a police officer in a van showed up and blocked my view and ordered me to find another way to go.

I turned around and saw that there were multiple cars behind me. While I drove back, I opened my window and flashed my headlights at them and stuck my arm out the window and signaled them to turn around. I ended up going through a residential area that from the looks of it, had been hit pretty hard. I saw many large downed trees, some of them were uprooted and others snapped in half at the trunk. It was not an easy, relaxing drive. I had to meander through a neighborhood that I didn't know, that had winding roads.

Eventually I ended up on Mill Road, which was flooded. There was about 4-6 inches of water and the road was littered with people's cars that had died while trying to get through. Luckily, I felt safe because I was in my trusty new Subaru Outback with a 6 speed manual and 8.9 inches of ground clearance. I mostly saw people driving big SUVs and trucks. I remember at one point I was driving south and the car that I had passed that was going north had left such a large wake in the waves that when they hit my car they lapped up onto the hood. My air conditioning was on and I was smelling low tide in my car. I didn't realize it at first, but the water I was driving in was sea water. I couldn't believe it.

I kept going, meandering around abandoned cars and downed tree branches until I got close to my house. The drive was perilous. I am not talking about the debris or the flooded roads. I am talking about being on the same road as everyone else who is in shock, emotionally compromised, and having the act of driving being the last thing that they are paying attention to. I am also talking about driving on the same road with these people when not only are there no traffic lights, but everyone knows that the red light cameras are not functioning and that the police have more important things to do at the moment than stop someone for a traffic infringement. I have never seen people driving with such blatant disregard for not only their own safety, but the safety and wellbeing of others; I was constantly amazed by what I was watching. They were driving like crazy people. I narrowly missed being involved in multiple accidents just while I was on my way to the house.

I remember pulling over to the side of the road to collect my thoughts before I continued on my journey to reach my destination, home. While pulled over I started to listen to a song I had downloaded onto my phone. This song became a treatment for my anxiety, stress and self-doubt. The song is called "Home," and was sung by Phillip Phillips. The combination of its lyrics and the tone of his voice were cathartic and helped me to relax and keep a positive frame of mind. At times it seemed like the song was written for us to bring us strength. The lyrics go as follows: "Hold on to me as we go, as we roll down this unfamiliar road, and although this wave is stringing us along, just know you're not alone, 'cause I'm going to make this place your home. Settle down, it'll all be clear, don't pay no mind to the demons, they fill you with fear, the trouble might drag you down, if you get lost, you can always be found."

I must have listened to that song a thousand times. I found its lyrics to have profound meaning to me. I kept listening to it and having in mind that the one who was going to "make this place my home" and "hold on to me as we go" was the Rebono Shel Olam (G-D). Every time I heard those lyrics "hold on to me as we go" I had in mind the famous story with the person who had a hard life filled with trials and tribulations and had tiynas (a point of contention) against Hashem (G-D) when he goes up to shamayim (heaven). He asks, where were You Rebono Shel Olam (G-D) when I needed You, my life was so hard, why didn't You help me when I needed You? And the Rebono Shel Olam shows him what was happening to him behind the scenes. The man sees that when times were good, there were 2 sets of footprints next to each other everywhere he went, but when times got tough there were only

1 set of footprints. The man shouts at the Rebono Shel Olam, why are You showing me this? You are proving my point. Why was there only 1 set of footprints when I needed Your help the most, why did You leave me alone in my darkest hours? And the Rebono Shel Olam answers him, those were My foot prints. I was carrying you on my back through the tough times. That is what the lyrics "hold on to me as we go" meant to me. I was asking the Rebono Shel Olam to let me hold on to Him because I desperately needed His help to go on. In the weeks and months to come I am sure that there were many times when I would only see 1 set of foot prints.

When I started to drive again I couldn't believe my eyes. I saw that one of the driveways that were between 2 houses on Seagirt Blvd had a boat parked in it. I knew that it wasn't their boat and that it wasn't there before the storm because I had never seen it there before. I thought that it was amazing that it ended up in the driveway between the 2 houses and causing no damage instead of crashing into one of the houses and ending up in their living room.

The boat that was pulled away from where the flood waters had deposited it between two houses

I noticed that there was a larger police presence in my neighborhood than I had ever seen. Everywhere I looked, there were either police cars parked on the median, police officers walking on the sidewalks, or patrolling the neighborhood. It was nice to see their presence in the neighborhood because I knew that they were there to avoid people coming from outside the Jewish community and looting. On a side note, this isn't the first time that I had seen an increased police presence in my neighborhood. During the east coast blackout of 2003 the police practically made a border of police cars surrounding our community. Every street that went from the rough side of Far Rockaway into our own was blocked off and manned to make sure that no one was allowed to enter our own little safe haven to avoid looting and keep us safe.

Back to my trip home. I decided to postpone my arrival at our house because I was not yet emotionally ready to see it. I decided to drive around the neighborhood and check on my friends' houses and apartments instead. There were several trees that had been knocked down and blocking roads so I had to meander through the neighborhood to get where I was going. Baruch Hashem all of my friends' houses at least appeared to be alright. Then I went back to Seagirt Blvd to check on one more families' house on my way to my own, Rabbi and Rebbetzin Freed's house. They were the people whose house I was most worried about. They live on Seagirt Blvd and would have taken the brunt of the hurricane's powerful surge. I was elated to see that their house was not only there but appeared to be structurally intact from the outside. Unfortunately, I later found out that wasn't the case. They had tremendous structural and content damage inside. After leaving their house I continued down the road and made a death defying right turn on Beach 9th street. The intersection of Beach 9th street and Seagirt Blvd is a very busy intersection and all of the traffic lights were not working due to the power outage. Then I was approaching the next turn, which would lead me to my house at the end of the dead end.

I saw debris in the street.

SEEING THE HOUSE
FOR THE FIRST TIME

As far as foreshadowing goes, the visible debris that was on the main road was only the foreshadow of what I was about to bear witness to. While I was turning onto my street, I noticed that my neighbor on the corner was missing sections of her wooden fence and it looked like one of my kids plastic climbing toys was in her yard. I kept going down my block and about two thirds of the way down the street, I hit water. After seeing the water, the first thing that I noticed was the 2 cars that were at the end of the block before the storm. One of them was where it was left. The other was a compact sized car and had floated about a quarter of the way up the block and was perpendicular to the direction that it was originally situated.

The block was eerily quiet. Between no traffic, no airplanes over head, and no power, if I didn't know better, I would have thought that I had lost my hearing. I slowly drove through the ever deepening residual sea water and was watching the enormous wake that my car was causing. It was a bizarre and frightening experience hearing the water lapping up against the floor of my car. It was disconcerting to say the least. I davened that the water wouldn't be too deep and that my car would successfully be able to ford the deep water. Baruch Hashem my car made it through the deepest parts of the water unscathed and my feet were not getting wet.

The debris that was left on the corner of our street from when the water had subsided

I pulled into the driveway which was slightly higher than the street level and the water was only about 7 or 8 inches deep. Before I disembarked the USS Subaru I put on my waterproof boots and prepared myself to finally get to my house. My stomach was in knots. I remember breaking out in a cold sweat and felt like throwing up. I listened to "Home" a few times at a very high volume and finally built up enough courage to actually leave my safe haven in my car.

I opened the door. I pensively took my left foot and started to move it out of the car, while still gripping the steering wheel. I slowly lowered my foot into the water searching for the bottom. It took so long to reach the bottom and have the sole of my boot reach the driveway that I it seemed to be 10 feet deep. I audibly exhaled and felt some stress melt off of me. Now that I had my own foot in my own driveway, I was finally home. It took me significantly less time to bring myself to put my right foot into the water and actually step out of the car and close the car door behind me. I was frozen for a few minutes while I processed what I was experiencing. Hearing it from other people and seeing it on the news is definitely not the same thing as seeing it with my own eyes and feeling the pressure if the deep water being exerted on the outside of my boots.

The diminished lake between our house and our neighbors across the street that at its deepest was approximately 7 feet deep

It looked like I had arrived at a house boat that resembled my house. Besides the water, the first thing that I noticed was my kids' toys that were caught in my poor aravos plants that get harvested every year for Sukkos.

Our remaining toys that were caught in our aravos which kept them from floating away

Most of our outdoor toys, like the climbing cube, Little Tykes picnic table, riding toys and multiple other toys were all caught in 2 mortally wounded aravos plants. I was saddened to see the state of my aravos plants but I was able to see that most of our toys were still there because they were tangled in its branches. I am not saying that I understand the reason why Hashem does the things that He does, but I would like to think that the toys were caught in those specific aravos bushes as a form of meeda kineged meeda (measure for measure) because of the purpose that those aravos bushed served. They exist strictly for chinuch (educational) purposes. I would venture to say that those bushes produce several hundred viable sets of aravos anually. I never sell them or give them to people to sell. A pair of scissors is tied to my fence. That way, friends or people who are either embarrassed to take due to their personal financial situation or people who only have time late at night or while I am at work can take at their leisure. They are also given away for free to Rabbis in the community and people who can't afford to buy them whether it is due to financial hardship or because they were blessed with large families and buying that many sets becomes very expensive especially when added to the normal additional expenses of the Yom Tov(holiday). I like to think that because their main purpose was chesed, Hashem used them to show me chesed.

It was of the utmost importance to at least make an attempt to keep a positive frame of mind and look for the good in everything, especially in this situation. Usually it didn't work while we were in the thick of it, but I am able to appreciate more of the positive aspects and outcomes now when I look back on them. I remember starting to walk down the driveway and head toward the stairs to enter the house. I felt like the wind had been knocked out of me; like my feet were cemented to the floor. I remember dragging my feet under the water for the first couple of steps towards the house when I realized that the water was too high for that. It was starting to come in over the top of my boots, that's when I started to march to try to keep my shoes and socks as dry as possible. Kerplunk splask kerplunk splash kerplunk splash. With each step that I had to pull my boots out of the water and plunge it back in for the next step I felt like my feet were made out of lead.

I needed help to get through this. I felt like I was fading. I was emotionally and physically drained. I remember having a short but intense conversation with the Rebono Shel Olam at that moment. I was standing outside my house in about 11 inches of muck that was comprised of a disgusting mixture of sea water, rain water, mud, sewage, oil, gasoline, cleaning chemicals and debris of all kinds. I remember beginning to cry and stopping myself. I was so physically drained from my emotional state that I was worried that if I would cry, I would have had nothing else to give. I wanted to hold it together. I needed to hold it together. I had trouble speaking. I was trying but because I was holding back tears I couldn't get a word out. Finally I started to hum the tune to esah einie. I hummed that niggun for a good 2 or 3 minutes with intense kavana before I was able to get a word out, and they would only come out in the form of that niggun whose words were replaced with the words of my tefilah. I was asking for strength and fortitude and the endurance to continue to be able to do what needs to be done. I was also singing praises of thanks to Hashem for seyata deshmaya for changing my mind about staying home and for keeping my family safe.

After a few minutes of psyching myself up, I started to walk up the stairs that lead to the entrance of my house. That first step felt strange. I slowly raised my foot out of the water, like I was getting out of a bath tub and suddenly had the strangest sensation of calmness. As soon as I was out of the water for a split second my troubles vanished and I felt like I was actually home on a normal day and that life was going to go on as normal. Just standing there without being wet, one hand on the handrail and the other touching the stucco finish of my house; I could feel my tension start to melt away. Out of habit I even checked the mail in the mailbox. I turned around and looked at the land around my house once more. My house is surrounded on 2 sides by wetlands that are full of bulrushes which usually grow to be a beautiful fifteen foot tall wall of green surrounding my yard. I noticed that they were bent, not broken. This gave me hope that *gom zeh yavore* (this too shall pass) and just like the bent stalks of the bull rushes were not broken and will grow back to their full beauty, so shall we.

I grabbed the house keys from my pocke,t where they were put for safe keeping to avoid them falling into the salt water lake that surrounded my house. I had trouble selecting the house key because my hands were shaking. All of a sudden my fears came back to the forefront of my mind. I realized that I was about to find out what had happened to my house and I was petrified to see what I was about to be exposed to and how it was going to affect my life. At that moment I wished that I wasn't alone; that I had someone to physically be there with me for emotional support.

I put the key into the deadbolt and turned it slowly. When I finally heard the click of the deadbolt when I unlocked it, it felt like a shock that quickly permeated my entire body. The door didn't open automatically like it had always done before. I thought that this was an ominous sign of the things to come once I opened the door to see what had happened to our home. Was the door stuck? Did the first floor flood out and something like the refrigerator was wedged behind the door? I did my best to try to calm the thoughts in my head and I took a deep breath, asked Hashem to give me strength and I tried to open the door again. The door wouldn't budge. I checked the locks a few times and they were unlocked. Was I losing my mind? Was the stress too much for me?

I finally had enough. I turned the door knob and shoulder checked the door as if I was a hockey player. I finally opened about 15 inches and abruptly stopped when the bottom of the door wedged itself on the living room floor like a ship running aground and I hit my head on the door. I was very confused and had trouble processing what had just happened. I couldn't even close the door. The living room floor was so warped from being saturated with seawater that the door was stuck. The house stank of stagnant sea water, mildew, and sewage. I slowly sidled my way in to the house between the door post and the immovable door and just stood there slack jawed. I could see that everything on the floor was wet but that everything that was more than one foot above the floor seemed to be ok. I didn't even think of the basement at that time. I was just elated that most of the first floor appeared to be fine.

I quickly ran upstairs to see if anything had happened to our bedrooms. Baruch Hashem, everything upstairs was unscathed. All of the windows seemed to be intact and the roof hadn't leaked and the floors weren't wet. I sat at the top of the stairs and cradled my face in my comforting hands and thanked Hashem for protecting our bedrooms and most of the first floor. I remember daring to start to get a positive feeling, an uplifting feeling that maybe we were at the turning point and that we would be able to come home soon.

At that point I went downstairs and went out of the back door to the house to check on the backyard. While I was on the way to the back door, I noticed that the kitchen and bathroom floors were covered with a thin layer of sand that made the floor very slippery. I had to remove the generator from its spot by the back door and put it into the kitchen and opened the back door. To my amazement, my shed, deck, and new barbecue grill were still there. The barbecue had been pushed to the other side of the deck and was precariously wedged at the top of the stairs that lead down to the ground level of the back yard but Baruch Hashem it didn't fall or float down the stairs.

Upon further inspection I noticed that the water line from the hurricanes surge was still visible on the back of the shed. Upon further inspection of the shed, I found that all of its contents except for two surf boards, three boogie boards, and a sled were ruined.

*The water line on the back of our shed that showed the height of the
surging flood waters when they were at their highest level*

I was having trouble comprehending that it was possible for the ocean to have risen that high and that my house still remained. I noticed that the garbage bag that I mistakenly left out on the deck to protect my sukkah walls from getting ruined by the rain had also kept it safe from the flood waters and the water had not penetrated it. I also noticed that my barbecue grills cover was missing and that the slide that was affixed to the deck was gone, only a gaping hole remained. I was unable to get into the shed at that time to check on its contents because our backyard is lower than our front yard so the water level back there was even higher.

Our old swing set which was now more suitable to be called a water park

When I looked at our swing set sitting in the new Meehan Ave salt water lake in my backyard I thought to myself that my kids would enjoy it even more this way. It was like a water park. At that point I received a phone call from Julie and Bubbs. They asked me to tell them what I saw, if I was safe, and when we could come home. I wasn't sure what to tell them. My dilemma was that I didn't want to tell them that things were worse than they were because I didn't want them to become overly depressed for no reason. On the other hand, I didn't want to understate the damage and have them get their hopes to high only to become depressed to find out that things were worse than I had mentioned.

I decided to tell them what I really thought. Taking a deep breath, I told them what I had seen and that unfortunately we weren't going back home any time soon. After I got off of the phone with them I started to go to the basement. Due to the fact that there was no electricity and no windows I needed to use flashlights to see what was going on in the basement. I grabbed the best and brightest flashlight we had and my camera and opened the door to the basement. I was immediately bombarded by the strong and concentrated stench of mold, stagnant sea water, sewage, and low tide that wafted out of the basement and I became nauseous instantaneously. With each step down toward the basement the smell became stronger and more potent. With each step I took going down the staircase I felt and heard the over saturated carpet on the stairs as the water was squeezed out beneath my boot. I couldn't believe what I was seeing. It looked like the aftermath of a monsoon.

Our belongings that were once stacked into neatly setup and organized shelving units, now strewn about haphazardly by Sandy's wrath

Where the ceiling had collapsed from the weight of the saturated sheet rock and where our washer and dryer ended up after floating around in the submerged basement

Our once orderly basement looked like a tornado had hit it. Before the storm, the basement was set up with plastic shelving units from floor to ceiling that were organized into categories. Apparently Hurricane Sandy had a very different idea about how the organization should have been done. Nothing was even close to being in the same vicinity of where it once was. Entire sections of the ceiling had collapsed, the washer and dryer were moved and rotated, and everything looked like it was thrown from its place in a haphazard fashion. I wanted to start the cleanup process but I didn't have the koach (strength) necessary for the task. I called Julie and told her what I had witnessed and experienced and said that I was coming back to my parents' home and that I was done for the day.

On the way home I decided to fill up my car with gasoline. Every gas station that I passed was either closed because they had no electricity to pump the gas or was mobbed with more cars than they could handle. The gas lines spilled out onto the streets. The lines went on for blocks and blocks. I decided to try to get gas near my parents' house where there wasn't any power outage in the hopes that I would be more successful in my quest. Luckily, I was able to get gas on Union Turnpike without having to wait on a line. It was the polar opposite of what I had just seen. The gas station had 6 working pumps and I was the only car there. I called Julie from the road and asked her to call the insurance companies and start the claim process.

When I got back to my parents' house I hugged my kids and wife and said "it will all be ok". Even if internally I wasn't so sure. I was immediately bombarded with a plethora of questions faster than I could give answers. I decided that I would be able to give them the answers that they were looking for in a way that was much less taxing on me. I took the memory card out of my camera and put it in the SD reader in my parents' 60 inch television. After all, a picture is worth a thousand words. As we went through the pictures that I had taken earlier I noticed that every time a new picture came on the screen at least 1 person would kvetch. An unfortunate side effect of seeing the destruction and mayhem on the screen was that Julie started to cry. She was sitting next to Bubbs, and Bubbs made her stand up and she gave her a big hug and rubbed her back and told her that "it will all be ok".

That night, both my wife and I couldn't sleep. We had too many things going through our minds. The stress and fear was all encompassing. When I thought that she was awake but needed an emotional shoulder to lean on I whispered "awake?". We have a rule. If you are awake and want to know if the other person is awake you don't call them by their name because sometimes that wakes them up and causes a lot of frustration and apologies that were not necessary, so we use the safe word "awake". So, she said yes, "I am awake. I can't get those pictures out of my mind. How are we going to recover from this?" I decided to put our mantra to good use, I said that "everything will be alright, we have each other." We stayed up for a while that night, expressing our fears and how it made us feel and consoling each other. Finally, I decided that I needed a drink to calm myself. Before I went upstairs to get a drink for myself I asked Julie if she could use one. She said "I thought you would never ask, yes please." While I was upstairs pouring myself a shot glass of bourbon and my wife chocolate liquor with some Ice, my cell phone rang. It was my Dad. He was calling to see how everything was going. After all, he was in China for business and had no idea of the days' events. His only information that he was able to obtain about the aftermath of the hurricane was from the Chinese coverage of the devastation and the internet. I told him what had happened and emailed him pictures. He expressed how sorry he was, not only for our losses, but for not being available to help with the cleanup. He also expressed his appreciation for us staying at their house to make sure that my mother AKA Bubbs was not alone. I said that he was welcome and that I was glad to make sure that she was safe and we got off of the phone. I brought our drinks downstairs and we tried to enjoy them and schmooze about anything that was not hurricane related. Eventually, after some more discussion and mutual consoling we fell asleep.

BACK TO WORK

The next morning I woke up earlier than usual because it was the first day after the hurricane that I was going to go back to work and my parents' house is further from Coney Island Hospital than our house. Would there be debris? Would the parking lot be flooded? I had no idea what to expect.

I looked at it as an adventure. There was no traffic anywhere. I made sure not to listen to the news and to only listen to music. I already knew that there was a hurricane and that there was a lot of damage. I didn't need to listen to the news where they would just go on and on talking about the same things over and over again.

I had to use the back entrance of the hospitals parking lot because the main entrance to was closed off and locked. I was able to get my normal parking spot. It felt like everything was going to fall into place. I couldn't live in my house but at lease everything else in my life was still going to go along as it did before the hurricane so there was still some semblance of normalcy. Coney Island Hospital is made up of a few buildings. For the purposes of this book I will only talk about the 2 main buildings that pertain to this story, the old building and the tower. The old building housed a few patient wards, offices, the dietary department, the labs, the operating rooms, the ER, dialysis, rehab, and a few other areas. The tower was the newer building that housed patients and it is attached to the old building. It was about 6:45 AM and about 40 degrees. I had parked and started to walk to the tower building so I could use their elevators and then walk inside to the old building to get to the Occupational therapy department as I usually did. While I was walking I tried to call Julie but I couldn't get reception. Apparently the power outage was affecting the cell towers in the area and I couldn't call Julie to tell her that I had arrived safely.

Normally at that time of the morning the lobby is empty except for security. When I opened the door to the lobby I was hit with a wall of sound. It was so loud that it was very difficult to discern individual voices. It was just one big plethora of shouting. The lobby was overflowing with people, all yelling and not sure what to do and where to go. It was chaos. There were many hurriedly made crude signs all over the elevators and the surrounding walls that were meant to tell people where they should report to. There were so many signs and they were all put up on the walls so haphazardly, that they were more confusing and frustrating than they were useful.

Baruch Hashem the new building had power because of its backup generators. They gave us light and heat and that was enough. I crammed into the crowded elevator and made my way up to the 3rd floor. When the elevator doors opened on the 3rd floor of the tower I was hoping that it would look like it usually does, nice and quiet. Nice and quiet couldn't be farther from what I was being exposed to. The halls were mobbed with nurses. Everyone was yelling to each other asking about sign in sheets and where they should report to. I fought my way through the crowd and made my way down the corridor where the patient's rooms were located.

It was a strange sight to see the patient rooms void of patients and replaced with staff members that were waiting to receive their marching orders. They were sitting on the chairs and beds and eating breakfast on the tables and at the sinks. As I walked further into the tower, I noticed different makeshift stations. They were set up with sign in sheets with the names of different hospitals on them. The hospital was having nurses sign in at Coney Island Hospital (Coney) and then deploying them to different hospitals via shuttle vans to keep them working so that they keep getting paid. It was also to assist the surrounding hospitals that absorbed our patients that were relocated.

I kept walking until I got to the double doors that lead to the old building where the Occupational therapy (OT) department was located. As soon as the doors opened I was met by a gust of frigid air. Apparently the new building had its generators working and providing heat, but the old building had both a basement and a sub-basement that had both been flooded and that knocked out the backup generators. There was no power or heat. The only way to walk around was to have a flash light. Luckily I keep an emergency flashlight in my car. I walked down the hall and finally got to the OT department and it was even colder because it was surrounded by large windows on 3 sides. I was the first one there. I kept trying to make cell phone calls to let Julie know what I had arrived safely, but there was just not enough reception to make a call. I tried from the landline phones but they were out of order because there was no power. I decided to text her and it finally worked.

Now I was happy because she wouldn't worry about me anymore. I had nothing to do and tried to not play games on my cell phone because I couldn't recharge it and I knew that the batteries would die quickly because it would constantly be searching for a signal. Instead of just sitting there and being bored I decided to take out my gemora and start my daf yomi for the day. While learning by flashlight in the cold I felt a real connection to the previous generation that learned by candle light. By the time I had finished the day's daf I was still the only one there. I decided to roam around the old building. I quickly found out that hospitals that have no lights, have no patients, have no heat, and are completely empty and silent are spooky placed to be when you are by yourself holding a flashlight.

The patientless and powerless halls of Coney Island Hospital

The hospital's emergency lights were the only lights on in the area

The cots in the physical therapy gym were remnants of the sleeping quarters for the teams of people who helped to care for and evacuate the patients from the hospital

It was so quiet that I was hearing the echoes from my foot steps and I was wearing rubber soled sneakers. I was having flashbacks from every scary movie I had ever seen. After spending about a half hour roaming around the building I decided to head back to the OT department to see if anyone had come to join me. My boss and a few of the other therapists were there. We all exchanged pleasantries and talked about what we had gone through. I found out that one of our therapists assisted with the evacuation of the patients because she lives about 5 minutes away from the hospital and came to work to help. I am the only one in my department that was dramatically affected by the hurricane. Other people just had to deal with traffic and the occasional blackout.

After schmoozing for a while we were tasked with combing the hospital for OT and PT wheelchairs that were utilized in the evacuation process and bringing them back to their respective locations. When we finished that undertaking we sat around a table and talking about how cold it was. Luckily the OT gym had a gas powered oven with a stove top. We decided to light all 4 burners and use them for heat and to make hot water for tea and coffee. We decided that the area was big enough that we wouldn't have a problem with carbon monoxide poisoning. It helped a little bit if you were close enough to the stove but not much. After doing nothing of any use for a while I decided to leave after lunch to go back to the house and start the cleanup process. Fortunately, my boss said that it was alright and I filled out the paperwork to leave early and I started my journey home.

My excursion would take me through some of the hardest hit areas that were on the southern coast line like Rockaway Beach, Belle Harbor, Arverne, and finally, Far Rockaway. I wasn't worried about getting stuck somewhere because I was driving my super Subaru Outback. Where others would get stuck, I would have the ground clearance and traction to get through. I had a cellphone holder that was dashboard mounted and adjustable which allowed me to put my cell phone in the cradle and have the camera pointed in front of me so I would be able to take pictures and video of what I was seeing without using my hands to hold it to let me focus on the task at hand of driving. I couldn't believe what I was seeing.

Piles of sand that were removed from the road to make peoples homes
more accessible

Where the beach's sand was extended by more than 1,000 feet and where a portion of the boardwalk in Rockaway Beach came to rest

Where the boardwalk in rockaway beach was ripped from its cement support structures

Flooded out streets in Rockaway Beach

I saw cars piled on top of each other, sand dunes in the street, sand covering the street to the point that it looked and felt like I was driving on the beach, peoples belongings out in the street and in their front yards, boats on the street and on lawns, and houses that were torn apart from either the downed trees or the tidal surge or both. I watched 4x4 after 4x4 getting bogged down in the muck, sand dunes, and piles of debris. I was very happy to be driving in my Subaru off-roading machine of awesomeness. I never got even close to becoming stuck no matter what was thrown at it. I decided to go around some areas because the sand dunes that were where the street used to be were between 3 and 4 feet high, and I was worried that they might be covering manholes that had their covers either shifted or removed altogether.

STARTING TO WORK ON THE HOUSE

When I made it through the veritable wilderness to my house I noticed that Baruch Hashem most of the water had been absorbed into the ground. Because I have a half submerges basement with a French drain, it would have been an exercise in futility to use the pump because the water level outside was at the same level as the water level inside the basement. A French drain is used in areas where the water table is higher than the basement floor in order to keep basements dry. A porous pipe is put under the basement floor going around the periphery. The pipes lead to a 33 gallon drum that is put into the floor so that the top is flush with the rest of the basements floors surface. A submersible pump is put into the bottom of the drum and when the water pours into it from the porous pipes and reaches a certain level the pump is activated and it pumps the water into another pipe that is connected to the sewer system.

I decided to use my generator to operate the pump that I had bought to get rid of the water from my basement. Baruch Hashem the pump started right up. Due to the fact that my basement has no doors or windows to the outside I had to put the generator on the deck in the back yard and have the extension cord go through the kitchen, through the dining room, down the stairs to the pump that I put into a 4 gallon plastic bucket that I drilled at least one hundred small holes in to make sure that debris didn't get sucked into the pumps motor and jam or break it. Twelve hundred gallons of mucky water per hour was flowing through a garden hose that went from the pump, up the stairs, through the dining room, out the window through the yard to the front of the house. There it flowed into the street and met up with the veritable river of water that was being pumped out of my neighbors' basements up the block.

My hose contributing to the river of water that was being pumped out from my neighbors basements

I asked my neighbor that I am semi attached to (my kids call him Uncle Frank) and his neighbor, who are both of African American descent, if they would like to plug their pumps into my generator. We really felt bad for the neighbors 2 houses down, because they were bailing out their basement with buckets. I figured that it would be a good opportunity to make a nice *Kiddush Hashem*. The only problem was that neither of them had a long enough extension cord. I went into my storage closet and found 2 long cords and for them to borrow. While the pump was doing its job, and doing it well, I was filling contractor garbage bags with our belongings from the basement and bringing them outside to be taken by the garbage men. Every once in a while I would need to take a mental health break and I would just sit on the soggy basement steps and just be frozen with mental exhaustion. I also took a few breaks and went down the block to see what the neighbors were up to and how they were doing. I needed to be around people for emotional support through proximity and shared experiences.

I let the pump do its job for a good 3 or 4 hours before I decided that I was exhausted and it was time to go back to my parents' house and take a good hot shower. I went to my neighbors and told them the time that I was going to shut off the generator and leave and that I was going to return the next day and that they were welcome to use our generator again.

Because things weren't bad enough, now not only was there a gas shortage, but it was getting worse. I don't remember exactly what caused the problem. It had to do with damaged refineries and docks that barges with gasoline would use to dock and unload the gasoline to supply the New York and New Jersey area. Whatever the root of the problem was, it didn't matter. We were still in a bad situation. Luckily I had only put 5 gallons of my 15 gallon stash into the generator so I had that 10 gallon cushion just in case. Our cars were also mostly filled, but I was worried. Even though my car has 6 gears and is a manual so it would get great gas mileage when driven prudently, I still had a long commute every day. I would start out in Queens, drive to Coney in Brooklyn, drive to our house in Far Rockaway, and then return back to my parents' house. I really wanted to avoid waiting on gas lines that were between 4 and 10 hours long, given that you were taking it for granted that you could even find a gas station that had both power and gasoline. I did the long commute to work and then the house to clean and back to my parents' house more times than I would like to remember.

On one of the trips to our house, Julie and Bubbs came to help me. While I was working in the basement, Julie and Bubbs were cleaning on the first floor. I heard Julie say "Oh My Gosh!" upstairs and then I heard her footsteps running toward the basement door. She came down stairs hiding something behind her back and said "guess what I found?". I told her that I wasn't really in the mood for guessing games, but she coaxed me to at least make an attempt. So I made some ridiculous guesses like a hippopotamus and a lamp shade. Finally she got frustrated and gave in and showed me my Shabbos tallis bag. I was so happy. I asked her where she found it. She told me that it was in the basket of the stroller and was untouched by the flood waters. That means that it was resting safely in the basket of the stroller and had flood waters less than an inch below it because the stroller was on the first floor. Yes, the tallis and siddur were important to me but they were replaceable. The real jewel was the tallis bag itself. It had belonged to my great grandfather with whom I share the same initials which are embroidered on it. A family heirloom like that is absolutely irreplaceable. I stopped what I was doing and Julie handed it to me and I held it close to me and brought it to my car to keep it safe and then went back into the house to continue cleaning.

Bubbs had a present for us. She gave me another pump and a hose. Once I drilled what seemed to be a million holes in another plastic bucket I set up the other pump and hose and we were now pumping 2,000 gallons of disgusting stagnant water and sludge per hour from the basement. That was the day that I realized that my electric box was still in the on position. I was worried that they would turn the electricity on without warning and my house would go up in flames because the electric box in the basement had been completely submerged in salt water. Combining electricity and salt water is not a good shidduch (match). There was still about 7 or 8 inches of that nauseating mucky water in my basement but I had to shut off that electric box as soon as possible. I literally climbed on my hands, knees and stomach at times over the contents of my basement like a soldier in a minefield until I finally made it to the electric box. Once I got there, I not only turned off the main switch, but I also turned off each and every secondary switch for good measure.

Once the box was turned off we went on bagging the garbage. Unfortunately, I reached my hands into the cold black murky water and pulled out the waterlogged tattered remains of a cardboard box. The problem wasn't the box itself but its contents which were priceless to Julie. It was the box that was full of about 50 or 60 benchers from her friends' weddings that she had amassed over the years. They were so waterlogged that they couldn't be saved and had to be brought to Shor Yoshuv and put into their shamos (damaged articles that have the name of Hashem written on them that need to be disposed of in a dignified manner) truck. Fortunately for us, that was all of our shamos. Unfortunately for the community, there was so much flood damage in other people's homes that they had to use a full sized trailer from an 18 wheeler truck to cart most of the shamos away.

TRIP TO THE HOSPITAL

Finally, it was Shabbos. What a long and taxing week. It seemed like an eternity. How I yearned for my precious Shabbos. We were looking forward to some good old fashion Shabbos menucha (rest), or so we thought. We had a beautiful Friday night Shabbos seuda (meal) filled with L'chiams that were made showing *hakaras ha tov* to the Reboneh Shelolum for keeping us safe and for my parents giving us a place to weather the storm and to each other for giving each other strength when we need it.

Due to my physical and emotional exhaustion I woke up late for davening (praying) on Shabbos morning and while I was scrambling to get dressed to get to shul, Julie was making trips to and from the first floor bringing things up and down the basement stairs to get ready for the Shabbos day seuda. Again Hashem intervened and the reason I woke up late was because unbeknownst to me; I was going to be needed.

One of Julie's trips down the stairs ended abruptly when her foot went through the front of the open toed slipper and she fell down the stairs and landed on the floor, bumping her lower back on every step on the way down. I had heard the loud impact. She was at the bottom of the stairs screaming for me. "JESSE, JESSE, I CAN'T MOVE!! MY LEGS ARE TINGLING AND I CANT MOVE!! HELP ME!!"

It was my worst nightmare. I deal with patients every day at Coney on the worst days of their lives. I see them when they are hospitalized for malignant cancer, fractured spines, broken bones, spinal cord injuries, and diseases and other afflictions whose consequences are so horrific that I don't want to talk about them. I thought that this couldn't happen to Julie. Not my Julie. I can't have to treat my wife like one of my patients.

I kept thinking of the worst case scenarios. Those and many other ideas like it swirled around in my head for what seemed to be an eternity but what was actually probably just a second or two. She was saying that she couldn't get up because of the intense blinding pain in her back. She couldn't even move because of it. I ran over to her and had to calm myself down. Which is never easy when you are looking down at the love of your life, while she is twisted and mangled at the bottom of a staircase crying for you to help her, with tears streaming down her face. She was asking Hashem to make everything alright and to help her.

I quickly forced myself out of the panicking losing my mind husband mode and went into my diagnostic trained professional mode, but first I said a quick internal tefilah (prayer) to Hashem, beseeching Him, saying that I need everything to be alright, I can't handle anything else right now. I crouched down on the floor next to her, and held her hand and told her that "everything will be alright; I won't allow it to be anything other than alright". I started to ask her what the pain feels like. Getting a description of how pain is being experienced is very important diagnostically. She said that it is an intense and sharp pain. I asked her if it is in one place or is it radiating. She said that it was localized to a specific area. She was afraid to move so I moved my hand around and asked her to let me know when my hand was on it. When she finally said that I had found it I felt the blood drain from my face, but I had to keep it together for Julie. I was worried because she was describing a strong pain on her lumbar spine and couldn't move because of the pain. I was thinking, but not willing to accept, that it had the possibility of being a spinal cord or vertebral injury. Baruch Hashem it was not, but I didn't know that at the time.

I started to do a full neurological evaluation on her, dotting all of my I's and making sure to cross all of my T's. This was the most important evaluation I had ever done or ever will do; I needed it to be thorough, perfect, comprehensive, and fast just in case we had to go to the hospital. I evaluated everything that I could think of from tone, to muscle strength, to sensation, to proprioception, to DTR's (deep tendon reflexes) and more. I even checked her visual fields just in case she hit her head and didn't realize it. I sighed a sigh of relief and said "Baruch Hashem, neurologically everything seems to be alright".

I looked up and realized that my two youngest daughters, Basya and Miriam had come downstairs at some point and were playing not even 3 feet away from where Julie and I were. They asked if Mommy was alright and Julie said that "Mommy is fine" and they smiled and continued playing with their dolls. Bubbs came down the stairs with an ice pack and Julie and I decided to try to have her stand. I knew that I could do it because at work I have transferred patients that weighed more than 3 times what Julie weighs.

As soon as we started to move she screamed "STOP!!" "I can't do this, the pain is too strong." I gently put her back in the same position she had been in sitting on the floor leaning on the staircase and decided that it was time to call Hatzala (a Jewish volunteer ambulance company). The first 2 Hatzala members that showed up were both friends of mine, Ross and Rabbi Palmer. Ross has been one of my best friends ever since we were about 5 or 6. Rabbi Palmer was introduced to me as a Rebbi (teacher) in Ezra Academy in my beginners level limuday kodesh (Jewish religious studies) class when I first made the switch from public school into yeshiva in 9th grade.

I told them what had happened and that I had done a comprehensive neurologic evaluation. I told them that my findings were that there was no spinal cord injury. As a precaution they put her on a back board and immobilized her neck and carried her out of the house and into the ambulance. Once we were in the ambulance they went through their standard evaluations and protocols.

Once they had finished their protocols we all started to schmooze. I started to schmooze with Rabbi Palmer about work and my worries about the gas shortage. He told me that as an active Hatzala member, he was able to use special gas lines in order to not have to wait on those horrendous lines. Once it was no longer an issue, I learned that Julie and I didn't have to wait on the gas lines because we were allowed to cut the lines and or use the specialized gas stations because we had picture ID's that proved that we are both direct care providers in hospitals. Rabbi Palmer told me that he got gas at least once per week and that if I had gas cans he would try to see if he would be able to fill them for us. I told him that I had three 5 gallon gas cans. He said that would be fine and whenever our gas cans were empty I should bring them to him at work and he and or his wife would wait on the lines in order to refill them for us. They said that they were in touch with a network of other people who were able to find out when the normal gas stations were getting their gasoline shipments which would minimize the waiting on the gas lines. He also mentioned that if he would keep the empty gas cans in his trunk then when he would go on Hatzala calls in the middle of the night, he would be able to look for gas stations with small or no lines because of the odd hours of the night that he would be returning from the Hatzala calls. Once they were filled he would call me to tell me when I could pick them up.

I jumped on the opportunity to avoid the gas lines and enthusiastically said, yes please. When we got to the hospital we were brought into the emergency room and were taken in and waited to be seen. Julie kept asking me what I thought it could be and if she was going to be alright. I said that it was probably just a bone bruise or a sore muscle that was now inflamed.

She was very uncomfortable while on the backboard with the head restraint and kept beseeching the Reboneh Shel Olum to help her and make sure that she was okay. Eventually the nurse came over and took her vitals and soon after that the doctor came over and I told her what I do for a living and that I had done the neurological exams and my Hatzala friends also said that they didn't think it's a spinal cord injury from what they were able to gather from the presenting symptoms. The Doctor did her own exam, as is the normal protocol, and said that it was a bad bruise with some inflammation right next to her spine and that it would be painful for a while but would get better on its own with the help of some anti-inflammatories, pain killers and ice.

Whether it was halachically (according to Jewish law) permissible or not I am not sure but we were not in the clearest frame of mind and were worried about how it would affect the children knowing that Mommy had gotten hurt and had to go to the hospital and not knowing how she was doing, especially after all that we had all just gone through. We wanted, no, needed to get back to them. We had the nurse call a taxi for us. When the taxi showed up he took one look at us and saw that we were religious Jews and opened the doors for us. I transferred Julie into the taxicab which was a slow and painful process for her, and he closed the doors for us and took us back to Bubbe and Papa's house where he was paid using a sheenuiy(doing it in a different way) to try to avoid any direct issur (Torah prohibition). I told him that I didn't want any change back to minimize the issurim so he got a very nice tip. It was a long and painful journey to get from the cab into the house, but I assisted her as much as she needed while reassuring her that she was going to be alright.

When we crossed over the threshold of the house we were met with much fanfare by the kids. They were told to not hug mommy or jump all over her at least until she is sitting in a comfortable position on the recliner. I helped her get into the living room where Devora Nechama met us with an ice pack. In our house, dispensing ice packs is a common occurrence with Devora Nechama when someone is hurt. Julie sat in my fathers' (AKA Pappas') reclining arm chair. With the ice pack in place she was given a pain killer and an anti-inflammatory and she reclined and rested for quite a while. Baruch Hashem, we were finally back at my parents' home. The kids were constantly offering her something to eat and drink and things to read and blankets but all she wanted to do was lie there and wait for the pain to subside, which was completely understandable. Even though it was painful, she was able to get to the table with help to eat a dignified seuda with the rest of us. Even though she was in a tremendous amount of pain, she still wanted to be with us and feel normal. I think that a big motivator for her to get up and out of that recliner was to reassure the kids that "Mommy was alright". For the rest of the day I helped her get wherever she had to go until finally that night I assisted her with getting downstairs and getting into bed and lying down to go to sleep. Fortunately, she was able to sleep, partially because of the pain killers but also due to the emotional exhaustion that had taken place throughout the day. I was doing my best to at least appear to be doing well but inside I was falling apart. How many catastrophic events can a person withstand at the same time before they just fall to pieces? I was really pushing my limits but doing my best to at least appear to maintain strong and stable for my wife and kids.

About a week or so after the hurricane we had a snowstorm because the hurricane wasn't enough apparently. Where we were in Queens it wasn't the light fluffy kind of snow, it was at least 7 inches of heavy, densely packed snow and ice. Even though my dad was back from his business trip in China I decided that I earn some keebud av vi aim (honoring your parents) points and would clear the snow for my parents. After all, they were giving us a place to live and so much more. Instead of just using a shovel, I was going to try and do the whole job of clearing the snow using their snow blower. It would be a lot to clear but I figured that with the snow blower it would be fine. I had to clear the driveways as well as the sidewalk. I figured that because it was a heavy snow blower that weighed about 100 pound and was self-propelling that it would probably be easy. I was definitely wrong because it had rained first which caused the bottom layer of snow to turn into slush and ice. The tires on the snow blower could not get any traction. That was a big problem because it weighed about 100 pounds. I still had to clear the driveway that fit four cars comfortably as well as the sidewalk for a corner house. I had my work cut out for me. It felt as though I was pushing a plow in a field full of rocks. Even with wearing heavy boots that had deep tread I was still only able to move it only a few inches at a time with great difficulty. About 10 minutes into using the snow blower I had only been able to clear a small patch in the driveway and I noticed that I had a blinding pain in my right hand. At the time I assumed that it was because I wasn't wearing gloves and I was working hard so I thought that it was just a cramp or small pulled muscle. I put on a pair of gloves and continued to attempt to use the snow blower and work through the pain. It took me over an hour of relentless, grueling, and painful work but after about an hour and a half I finally finished clearing all of the snow. The pain was relentless and actually increased with time. This posed a large problem for me because it was my dominant hand and I am an occupational therapist who relies upon my hands in order to work. After the pain got to a certain point that I couldn't dismiss it anymore I knew I had to start to take care of the problem before it became chronic. I felt like the proverbial shoe makers son who had no shoes. I started to treat myself as if I was my own patient. I started going through the various evaluations and tests to try to diagnose exactly what I had done to my hand. Eventually through specialized testing I realized that I had sprained two muscles in my hand while using the snow blower. Unfortunately, through using my hand at work as well as participating in repetitive heavy lifting in my house I had turned two small sprains into two medium sized tears that would continue to get progressively worse if I did nothing about them. They were going to continue to deteriorate, and possibly turn in to a chronic injury, which I couldn't allow to happen because I need my hand not only for my job, but to be able to continue to do work on my house. It got so bad that I wasn't able to buckle my own belt or tie my own shoes without tremendous difficulty and excruciating pain. I decided to review my text books that teach how to make splints for different diagnoses and saw that the splints in the textbooks and review books were not adequate for what I needed them to accomplish. I decided to invent a new splint and I custom fitted it to my hand. After a few prototypes and revisions I designed a custom splint that would do exactly what I needed it to do which was immobilizing the injured muscles while allowing me to use my hand in the most functional manner possible. As soon as I affixed the newly designed splint I immediately felt tremendous relief. It was truly a mechiyah to not be in constant intense pain.

After utilizing the splint for about 3 1/2 weeks I began to notice that my symptoms were almost gone and that I had minimal pain. At that point I decided to discontinue the use of the splint while continuing to treat my hand using various treatment methods and exercises. I was able to function without the use of the split. Baruch Hashem after about two months of not wearing the splint all of the pain is gone and my hand is back to normal.

KLAL YISROEL

Baruch Hashem Julie started to feel a little bit better and she decided that she wanted to go to the house with me. I told her that it would be better for her to stay at my parents' house and rest and that when she was doing much better, I would love to have her at the house helping me. I decided that I was going to go to the house and do a lot of work and really start to make a difference. I brought out the generator and Baruch Hashem it started up right away and I plugged in my team of beautiful 2,000 combined gallons per hour pumps and got to work. After a few minutes, the same neighbors whom I had let plug their pumps into my generator came knocking at the door to ask if they could do it again. I told them that they didn't have to ask anymore and that if my generator is on they can just come and plug in whatever they need without asking me. They thanked me and continued to work on their own houses. After schlepping 2 very heavy contractor garbage bags that were filled to capacity I just sat down on the ground and began to give in to my emotions and started to feel hopeless. I was at my wits end. It seemed like no matter how much stuff I schlepped out of the basement I never even made a dent, after all, there was a lot of stuff down there and for the overwhelming majority of the time I was doing it alone. I remember this next part vividly. I received a text message at 10:43AM on November 4th (which will forever be embedded in my mind as the day that Hashem made sure that I knew that He had a real feeling of ahava (love) for me. Unfortunately I was too depressed to take my cellphone out of its case to check who it was from or what it was about. 2 minutes later, my cellphone reminded me that I had an unopened text message so I decided to check it this time just in case it had to do with Julie. Baruch Hashem I decided to check it. It was from one of my best friend's mother who lives in Florida. She was letting me know about an email that she had received from a Jewish organization that was asking people to come too Far Rockaway to help with the cleanup effort in any way that they can. It went on to say that there was an organization called Achiezer, and they were setting up their base of operations in Far Rockaway in Yeshiva Shor Yoshuv in the dining room. They were organizing people to come to Sandy victims houses and volunteer to help in any way that they are asked to if possible. I replied, "thank you so much" to her and went straight to Shor Yoshuv to see what kind of help I could get.

When I pulled up to Shor Yoshuv I found the parking lot to be mostly full. I thought to myself that a full parking lot was imyeertza Hashem a good sign that I was hopefully going to go back to my house with a nice sized chevra (group of friends) to help me. I walked into the dining room and saw that the place was abuzz with people with cellphones and walkie-talkies sitting at tables with pads and paper telling people where to go and what they will need with them and many other tzadeekim (righteous people) who were there with their boots on, work gloves hanging out of their pockets, and yeitzer tovs (good inclination) in high gear looking to earn some zechus for olumhabah. I didn't know where to go and who to speak to. All that I knew, was that I needed help. I decided to go over to a man sitting behind one of the tables that was closest to me and told him that I had heard that an organization called Achiezer was organizing volunteers to help Sandy victims. He asked me if I was a volunteer or someone who needed some help. I told him that I was looking for all of the help I can find. He said "wait a minute, let me check my list and see who I have to send right now". At that moment, the group of 8 tzadeekim that were hovering around his table just waiting for the opportunity to do a mitzvah with zereezus spoke up and said "what about us? Can we go?" To which the man behind the desk said "Yofie (beautiful), go for it". They asked me what kind of work I needed help with. I told them about the state of the basement and that I needed help cleaning it out. They said "let's go, you lead the way". I have never felt such a feeling of pride in my community and I said out loud how happy I am to be part of such a beautiful religion and thanked Hashem for this beautiful example of seeyata deshma-ya. As soon as I got into my car I called Julie and told her what happened. I heard her crying tears of joy which unfortunately caused some tears of pain because of her back injury. I apologized for causing her any pain but she said that it was alright, there is more joy than pain and made me continue telling her what was happening. I was so excited while I was telling her about Hashem's chesed that we were receiving that I was talking a mile a minute. I felt so elated at that moment, I felt like I could fly. I was actually shaking. I left the parking lot with the other people behind me in their cars. We pulled up to the house in what can only be described as the most beautiful caravan I have ever seen, let alone been apart of. I found it interesting how we had left our house before the storm in a small and downtrodden caravan of 2 and was returning to our house with a larger caravan of 4 cars with uplifted spirits to fix the house. Everyone came into the house with me and I noticed that they were all wearing dress shirts, slacks, and dress shoes. I asked them if they were sure that they could help me dressed like that. Some of them said that it wasn't a problem and others asked for garbage bags to put over their shoes and to protect the bottom half of their pants. Baruch Hashem I had plenty of contractor bags, flashlights, batteries, rubber gloves, and face masks to protect our lungs from the mold and noxious fumes in the basement. We worked at a break neck pace to fill the bags, bring them upstairs, and bring them outside. During the course of cleaning in the basement I added some gasoline to the generator and grabbed a pad and pen and put it on the dining room table and asked everyone who was there to please write down their names, phone numbers, and addresses. That way I could either invite people for Shabbos meals or send thank you cards, or send shaloc manos. I wanted to do something to show my *hakaras ha tov*. At that point one of the guys there told me his name but I had so many things on my mind and I was so busy that I didn't catch his name. I asked him to please write it down because I wasn't going to be able to retain his name in my memory. I noticed that when I said that everyone that was within earshot smiled. I wasn't sure why they were smiling but I politely asked him to please write down his name and other information because there was just no way that I was going to remember it. He put down the garbage bag that he was holding and smiled at me and said "you won't remember my name? It's Klal Yisroel". To which I replied, I appreciate that but I really want to show *hakaras ha tov* for the wonderful thing that you guys are doing for me. He replied "Klal Yisroel" is enough recognition for me. All of the other guys there said "that goes for me to". I choked up and almost cried right there and then in front of 8 perfect strangers that took time out of their busy lives to wade through some of the most disgusting and vile muck that I have ever seen and smelled before just to help me because I was a Yid. I was so touched. I thought to myself, "so this is what it means to be a Yid, a member of an exclusive club whose members would do anything for a perfect stranger just because he is a Yid. Together we quickly accomplished a tremendous amount over the next hour or so. At that point I heard grumblings from them about their cold and wet feet. At that point I told them about what an unbelievable mitzvah they had undertaken and how much I appreciated it but I didn't want to see them getting sick. I suggested that they stop and go and help another family whose house is dry and I call Achiezer and ask for the assistance of another group of selfless tzadeekim with water proof boots to come over and pick up where they had left off. After all, Achiezer had no shortage of Yidden who were Tzadeekim who only wanted to help as many people as they could. While they were leaving I was schmoozing with them and asking them where they were from. I had people from Monsey, Brooklyn, main land Queens, Far Rockaway, the Five Towns, and Baltimore that only came in to help out. They said that they were on their way to help other people empty out their first floor of their house because it wasn't wet. I thanked them more copiously than I have ever thanked someone in my life. I couldn't find the proper words to express how I felt about this wonderful mitzvah that they have undertaken, but I did the best that I could in showing my *hakaras ha tov*. When they pulled away they wished my good mazal and hatzlocha. I just stood there in the middle of the street watching them leave. I couldn't grasp what had just happened, I was speechless. I called Achiezer again and mentioned what had just happened and thanked them for it. I also requested another group that had water proof boots and was prepared for heavy lifting. They said, sure and took my information down and said that they would be at my house shortly. About 15 minutes later I heard a knock on the door. This time there were 8 guys wear-

ing boots and heavier clothing than the previous group and they came prepared with their own contractor bags, gloves, and air filtering masks. This
group was different from the first. There were some families represented by
multiple generations that wanted to help. It was a beautiful thing to see that
the older generation wanted the younger generation to not only watch them
put what they preach into practice but to take part in it. These guys had already worked as a team helping other people so they had a good system for
working efficiently and quickly. They made an assembly line and worked
faster than I thought was possible. Again, I tried to get their names and information like I had tried with the previous group. And again I was met with
the same response; "Klal Yisroel". Working as a team we only needed about
an hour and a half to do what would have easily taken me 3 or 4 weeks to do
on my own. While I was bringing out 2 full contractor bags I was outside
walking on the deck to bring them into the back yard I heard "Mr. Jesse, Mr.
Jesse, over here". I looked to my right and it was my neighbor from 2 doors
down. She was standing in her backyard with her 2 sons. She asked me if they
could help me carry things out of my house. She said, and I will never forget
how uncomfortable I was when she said this, "I have 2 young black backs
here (patting her sons on the back while she said it) to help you move your
things out of your house". I felt so uncomfortable; I didn't know if it was a
"racist" test. Should I acknowledge what she said or pretend that I didn't hear
it? I wasn't sure what to do so I took a deep and uneasy breath and said "I
don't care if their backs are black, white, purple, poke a dot or blue, I will take
all the help that I can get from where ever I can get it" and I thanked her and
them. They worked hard just like the rest of us and were very courteous and
polite. They asked what kind of help we needed and I told them, do whatever you see everyone else doing. When the Jewish crew was finished helping
me they left to go help another family who needed it. I was completely and
utterly blown away. I went back into the basement to see it once more. All of
our belongings were now out in the yard and only 5 or 6 inches of water remained even though the pumps were still going.

The first load of garbage from the basement that was put out for the garbage men

Some of the tzadeekim who helped us to empty the basement of our destroyed belongings

A portion of our ruined belongings once they had been taken out of the basement and put into the backyard

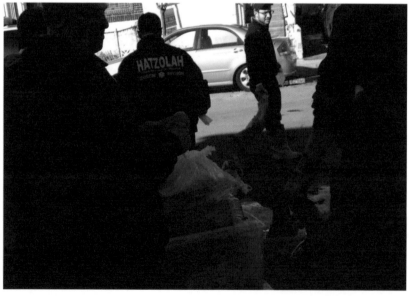

More of the tzadeekim who helped us and many families like ours to empty our basement

I was on a spiritual high like I have never experienced before but my body was just about spent. Even though I was exhausted from the events of the day I wanted to finish removing the little bit of debris that what left as well as get rid of the remaining water in the basement. At this point I was alone and knew that if I was going to do this alone that I would not have finished doing everything because without the support of a friend I would have just quit. I sent a text message to a bunch of my friends to see if anyone was available to come to the house and give me a hand. Everyone seemed to respond that they were either at work or unable to come over. I thought that I was going to have to try to do it myself. A few minutes later one of my friends texted me back saying that he was able to come over because he was not busy at the moment. Avrumie Biyagitz said that it would be his pleasure to come and help and asked if there was anything that I needed. I responded and told him that I need some batteries for the flashlights if he has a few to spare. He said that he would bring some and that he would be right over and he had about an hour or so that he could spend helping me with the basement. We first grabbed the larger pieces of left over debris and put them into contractor garbage bags and when we were finished with the larger pieces of garbage we moved on to the smaller pieces which we needed a broom and shovel to pick up. The smaller pieces were primarily consisted of broken pieces of glass, nails, broken pieces of plastic, and metal. We ended up filling another five or six contractor garbage bags and then got to work on the water. It was not as simple as putting the pumps in place and letting them do their job because the pump needed the water to be at least a half inch deep to get sucked up by the pump and pumped outside. We ended up using brooms to make waves in the water to make its depth more than a half inch when it would make contact with the pumps to get them to work. Being hunched over because my basement is 5'4" tall did not help things. Every time we would sweep the water toward the pump it would gurgle for a little bit and remove what was probably only a cup or so of water. It was painstaking repetitive labor that was not enjoyable but it was better to do with a friend than by myself. By the time he had to leave we had gotten rid of about 95% of the remaining water. To him it was just picking up some garbage and using a broom for a while while in a disgusting basement to help a friend. For me it was more than that.

It was cathartic knowing that a friend gave up his time to be in this dungeon of a basement helping me. The work that we accomplished together in the basement over that hour was more than I would've been able to do by myself in three or four hours of solitary work. I decided to call it a day and went back to my parents' house to rejoin my family and tell them the stories of the tzadeekim that I met that day. I couldn't wait to tell them everything. I was bursting at the seams with excitement. I couldn't wait any longer I had to tell someone what happened, after all, it was one of the most beautiful things I had ever heard of and I can't believe that I was there to experience it. It made me think about all of the Gedolim (highly respected Rabbis) stories that you read and the tales of tzadeekim that you hear about in drashas (Rabbis sermons) that talk about how entire communities come together to help someone and do incredible things and remain anonymous to make sure that they don't get any kind of recognition. It made all of those stories that I had heard and read more real to me because I could relate to them now. I finally gave in about 2 minutes later and while I was driving home I called my wife and told her the day's stories. I could hear her tearing up over the phone and I began to emotionally break down as well. It was such a powerful experience that when I heard her crying it started to penetrate me. I was finally realizing and appreciating what the Reboneh Shelolum had done for us. I remember hearing my wife say in a soft and cracking voice while she was crying "Hashem really does Love us, I can't believe that he did that for us. What did we do to possibly deserve all of this special treatment?". When I got back to my parents' house I was met by a fantastic group hug from D, Basya, and Miriam. They were telling me that they had heard the story from Mommy but wanted to hear it again from me. I told them that I was going to take a shower and wash off the day and when I come back upstairs for dinner I would tell the story again at the dinner table.

Later on, after my shower when I came to the table for dinner I was exhausted. I practically had to drag my feet up the stairs. After sitting down I started to regale my family with the tales of the tzadikim that I had met throughout the day. While telling them what had happened I felt that rush of emuna (belief in Hashem) surge through my veins. The surge of emuna turned into excitement and I was infused with a second wind of energy which made the retelling of the story animated instead of monotone. While I was telling them what had happened I was watching my daughters to see what their reactions were going to be. I watched their faces light up and their eyes widen and they kept asking me "then what happened" and "what did they do next?" When I had finished my tales of the day, they were upset that I wasn't able to get any of their names because they wanted to meet them and have them for Shabbos meals and tell their children how amazing their fathers and brothers are. I was so proud of my girls at that moment. All they wanted to do was express their *hakaras ha tov*. And then my oldest, Devora Nechama, said that if there is ever another storm that she wants to come and help other people, and then Basya and Miriam joined in and said that they want to help to. I said that imyeertza Hashem there won't be another storm but if there is, I am sure that anyone would be lucky to have them as there helpers.

The next day at Coney I had a new job to do. Now that the phone and computer systems were working we had to cancel all of our patients' appointments and document that they were being canceled due to the hospital being closed from Hurricane Sandy damage. We also had to call the patients to make sure that they didn't go through the perilous trip to come to the hospital for treatment. Some of the therapists were starting to be deployed to other local hospitals to not only treat some of our inpatient patients that were evacuated to other hospitals but also to earn their paychecks, that Baruch Hashem had not been disrupted at all. My boss was gracious enough to tell the administrators that were having us deployed that I was unavailable to be deployed at that time because I had work to do at Coney. I did some work here and there but the main reason that she did that was to help me be able to leave work early so that I could continue to work on my house while the sun was out. After all, it was November and my house had no heat so if I had to leave work at the normal time to go to the house it would have been much colder and I would have been much less productive. My boss was really in my corner, for which I will always be grateful.

BACK TO THE HOUSE

aruch Hashem, a few days later Julies back was feeling well enough
that she decided that the wanted to come with me to the house to
help with the cleanup. I was wary about her back, but happy to have
the company. I figured that if worse comes to worse, if her back can't
handle the constant bending over to pick things up, she would sit on the couch
and I would still have company. Our intentions were to begin to clean up and
remove the garbage from the first floor. While driving to the house I wanted to
make sure that Julie was prepared for what she was about to see. I wanted to minimize the shock as much as possible so we spoke in depth about what the house
and yard looked like. When we finally pulled up to the house Julie said "Oh my
gosh" and started to tear up and covered her mouth with her hand. I asked her
what was wrong. I knew that she was going to have an emotional response but I
wanted to make sure that the tension of the emotional response didn't cause her
to have a spasm in her back. She started to point at the back yard with the other
hand and said "look at all of our things, is it really all garbage?" Regrettably I had
to say "yes, unfortunately it is" and I explained that it had all been submerged and
bathed in the basement in toxic sludge. I told her that before we throw everything out I would go through most of it to see if there were things that could be
salvaged and then we went into the house. It had rained the previous night and
we came into the house to find that there were 4 or 5 inches of freezing cold water
mixed with other things in the basement. That is unfortunately one of the side
effects of having a French drain system that was damaged by a sewage back up
and not having power. As soon as the water level goes up in the ground, it backs
up into the house because the flow valve had been broken in the storm. I went

outside and emptied one of the gas cans into the generator because once we had a good cleaning rhythm going I didn't want to have to stop to refill the generator and throw us off. The generator wouldn't start. I tried to get it to start for about 10 minutes. No matter how hard I tried to get it started I couldn't get the motor to turn over and start. While I was trying to get it started Julie was looking at the instruction manual to see if there was anything to do. We must have checked every step in the manual at least 5 times to be thorough. I finally figured out what the problem was when I inspected the gas can that I had just emptied. Its seal was not intact and it was submerged in flood water several days earlier. I realized that some of the sea water was inside the gas can and it must be clogging up the generator. Now remember, gas was worth more than gold at this point. I had to flush out the generator that I had just topped off. That was 7 gallons of fuel that had to be discarded because I didn't think to check the valve around the nozzle of the gas can. I took a look at the generator and figured out how to drain it of its precious gasoline and grabbed a hose and detached the gas regulator and started to empty the tank. A few minutes later Julie took over the hose holding for me while its fuel tank drained.

Julie holding the hose which was draining our generator of the gasoline that was tainted with sea water

It took what seemed to be forever but what was probably only about seven or eight minutes. Once it was empty I reattached the gas regulator and we refilled the generator with more gasoline Baruch Hashem, it started right up; we put the rest into Julie's car to avoid her spending half of a day waiting in line at the gas station. I realize now what a silly thing dumping all seven gallons of gas was to do for a very simple reason that I learned in elementary school. Water is heavier than gasoline. We could have probably gotten away with only dumping a gallon or 2 but we were panicking and not thinking clearly and decided to just dump it all and start fresh to give us the best chance for success.

I just had an epiphany right this minute while I am typing this. Another beautiful seyata deshmaya moment brought to you by this stories sponsor, the Reboneh Shelolum. We used the same gas cans to both refilling the generator and to put fuel into our cars. Baruch Hashem that sea water made its way into our generator because I could easily drain my generator but if the saltwater got into one of our cars the consequences of getting mucky sea water in a car's gas tank would have been disastrous for us. It would have done damage to the car and caused it to stall and it would have definitely cost us time, money, and some of our little remaining sanity to get it taken care of.

While Julie was cleaning and organizing the first floor, the generator was powering the pump that was removing the water from the basement. I was sorting the garbage in the back yard and bringing it to the front of the house. We were both very busy and working very hard. All of a sudden my neighbor from 2 houses down, who I was allowing to use the generator, who is a black woman, came into the backyard holding a 1 gallon gas can. She had told me that she waited for 4 hours to get it filled and then hitched a ride back to the house to be able to give me some gas to chip in because she was using my generator. She said that we bought the generator and were supplying the gasoline to power their pump and that it was the least she could do to help supply some of the gas. It was a beautiful gesture and I know that it was very hard and time consuming for her to do. I thanked her profusely and took the gas can, put it right into the generator and gave her the gas can back. For some reason, all of the things that we had brought out of the basement and put into the back yard seemed to be heavier now. I am not sure if it was because I was tired or if it was psychological because I was doing it by myself and didn't have an entire team helping me. Julie suggested that we separate all of our clothing that was ruined in the basement and in the shed and put it into separate garbage bags to be brought to my in-laws to try to wash in their washing machine which they had volunteered to do. It was greatly appreciated that they wanted to try to help us salvage what we could. Because the clothing in the contractor bags was still sopping wet I didn't want them in my car because I was worried that they would leak and I would never be able to get rid of that repulsive smell. I decided to attach my roof rack mounted storage bin to my car and use that to transport the bags of clothing to my in-laws house. The clothing in question was baby clothing, regular clothing, and my wife's maternity clothing. There were 9 contractor bags filled their capacity with clothing. We had high hopes that they could be saved because it would have cost a small fortune to replace it all. After all of the clothing was separated, everything else was put into contractor bags and then put on a 7 foot long toboggan style snow sled that I pulled through the yard to the driveway. It was difficult and painstaking work to not only sort the items into "keep" and "throw out" piles and bags, but to make sure that the bags weren't too heavy or over stuffed in order to avoid them ripping and spilling their contents on the lawn or in the driveway. I decided that it had to be done as soon as possible. I also knew that we would feel better when we would be able to come to the house and not be met by the sight of all of our things that we had to throw out strewn about in the yard in piles. Seeing how hard I was working, Julie kept asking me if she could help me. I kept telling her that I didn't want her to lift or drag anything heavy, because I was worried about jeopardizing her back's recovery, and that what she was doing inside was very important. All of the bags of garbage were finally in the driveway and just waiting for the garbage men to pick them up.

By the end of that day we were both exhausted and sore all over. We went back to my parents' house and spent some time with the kids, showered to wash the grime off and went to sleep nice and early.

The second load of garbage

The third load of garbage

After the girls had no school for a little while due to the damage that their school had sustained during the hurricane we received a phone call. We were told that TAG (Torah Academy for Girls) was gracious enough to offer the girls round trip rides on their bus for free. We later found out that they had also made that offer to other people who had become displaced from Far Rockaway to main land Queens. I can't begin to tell you what a relief that was. We weren't sure what we were going to do about getting the girls to school. I was leaving the house at 6:20 in the morning just to get to work on time. My parents' house was only about 3 or 4 miles away from where Julie works. That would have been an incredible schlep for Julie and she would have had to go to work late every day and miss important meetings every morning pertaining to the two wards that she is in charge of at the hospital; not to mention the added gasoline usage which would have made us have to wait on the gas lines, even with Rabbi Palmers help. My dad was away in China for business so no one was using his car. He had a full tank of gas and I thought that it would be a great idea to try to siphon the gas out of his car in hopes that by the time he got back the gas shortage would be over and he wouldn't be inconvenienced. I tried and tried but to no avail. I didn't know why it wasn't working. I did some research online and found out that every car that was made after 2002 had a gas filter to avoid debris from getting into the gas tank. Unfortunately it also worked as a siphoning deterrent. I guess it wasn't meant to be.

DR. LIGHTMAN

I noticed that my sinuses started to bother me and I knew that it was the beginning of a sinus infection. Unfortunately I get them often enough to recognize the symptoms. I told Julie that I was going to go to Dr. Lightman after work so that he could check it out and let me know if he thought that I needed a prescription for antibiotics. Julie told me that her back was still causing her a lot of pain and that she was almost out of pain killers and that I should ask him if she could get a prescription for a painkiller or muscle relaxer for her back while I was there. I told her that I would try. I called Dr. Lightmans' office number knowing full well that his office had been destroyed. I was hoping that there would be a message on his answering machine to let me know where to find him. Baruch Hashem there was a message saying that he was at his house seeing patients. I went over to his house late in the afternoon and it had already started to get a little dark outside. After parking in front of his house I noticed that there were no lights on inside the house except for what looked like a faint flashlight moving around in his dining room. I also noticed that the entire block had no lights on. Upon further inspection I noticed that he had a generator outside his house that was chained to a tree with its power cord going into the house but the generator was not on. I checked to see if it was either out of gas or if it had stalled and just needed to be restarted. It was out of gas. I went to the door and knocked. His wife opened the door and let me in. She had told me that he was with a patient at the moment and that he would be right with me. Inside his house it was cold and dark. He apparently had no heat or electricity. I could hear him coughing and sniffling while he was examining the other patient. He sounded congested and like he was really sick. When he was done treating the other patient he called me in to his examination room, formerly known as his dining room. To my surprise he was sitting at the head of his dining room table with a flashlight affixed to his forehead, wearing a sweater and surrounded by basic medical equipment and his prescription pad on the table. He asked me how we did with the mabul (flood). I told him what had happened and he said "Hashem yirachem" and asked how the rest of the family was holding up. So we were schmoozing and he told me about how the office was destroyed and how his pleas to FEMA and to the state for a mobile office trailer were not only denied, but ignored. He then told me that he was pretty much the only doctor who was working in the extended area and that other doctors were sending their patients to him because they didn't want to work during the crisis. I told him that that was the downside to having a beautiful neshama (soul) and that he is underappreciated as the tzadik that he is. He then told me that he had pneumonia but if he didn't treat patients, who would. I explained our medical needs and he gladly wrote both of us our prescriptions. I told him that I would try to get him some gasoline for his generator so he could at least heat his house. He jokingly told me that if I could do that he would write me prescriptions for anything that I want. I told him that it was the least I could do. Here he was suffering from sickness and cold temperatures and working 20 hour days because of all of the patients flocking to him when their own doctors abandoned them because of the hurricane. How could I not help him?

I knew that I had a full 5 gallon gas can at the house for my generator and my car was almost on empty. I was wary about giving the gas away because I might need it to put in my car. I decided to try to get gas at a local gas station on the way back to my parents' house so I could give him the 5 gallons so that he could at least have heat in his house for 6 or 7 hours. While I was driving on the 878 heading back to queens I noticed that there was a gas truck at the Mobil gas station on the corner of the 878 and Burnside and it was refilling the gas stations supply of gasoline. I noticed that the line for gas was only about 15 cars or so and I quickly slammed on the brakes and fishtailed a little bit while I quickly downshifted and drifted my car over to the other side of the 878 facing the other direction and got in line. The line didn't move for an hour and a half while it was being refilled. The line quickly grew behind me faster than I would have imagined possible.

The gas line that quickly appeared and grew behind my car

People were so bored that a bunch of the drivers of the other cars in line put their cars in park and turned them off and got out of their cars and sat by the side of the road and just hung out. Eventually the gas station was opened and the line started to move. When I got closer I saw that there were 10 police officers there to make sure that there wasn't a gas crazed stampede or riot. They were also directing traffic. This gas station had 16 pumps and the 2 that were right by the shopping centers' parking lot were designated as the gas can lines. Those 2 pumps were for the people that were lined up on foot with their gas cans that needed to fill them up. There must have been at least 50 people standing out there. Some had one 1 gallon gas can while others had a few 5 or 10 gallon gas cans. I was very pleasantly surprised to see that everyone was cooperating and not trying to jump the line. I even saw one of the cars ahead of me that had apparently ran out of gas while waiting on line, being pushed by perfect strangers that happened to be walking by.

Once I filled my car to the brim I went back to the house and got the 5 gallon gas can and brought it directly to Dr. Lightmans' house. He was so happy he gave me a big hug and jokingly asked me if I want that prescription for what ever I want now. I left his house with a real sense of accomplishment, like I had done something to help the unappreciated tzadik that he is. When I went to sleep that night, I felt really positive because I knew that he, his wife, and family were going to have heat in their house that night and that I was a part of it.

The next day when I went to the house I wanted to start up the generator and use it to power the pumps to remove some of the water that had come back into the basement from the rain that occurred the previous night. I couldn't get the generator to start. I tried for more than a half hour to get it started. I kept checking the manual to see if there was anything else for me to do, but there wasn't. Then I tried calling the company and asking them what I should do. They said to either send it back to them to be repaired or to try to return it to the store. I decided that for all of the money that I spent on this generator, I didn't want one that had to be refurbished after only ten and a half hours of use. I wanted a brand new one. All I had was the receipt. The box that it came with was washed away from the hurricanes tidal surge. I had heard that people were trying to return their generators to Lowe's and they weren't taking them back. I think that the reason that they weren't allowing people to return their generators was out of an overreaction. I don't agree with it but I can understand the logical argument from a business perspective. It is my opinion that Lowe's thinks that if they allow people to return their generators after a disaster occurs that it will send a message to people who either can't afford the item in question or who need the item in question during and immediately after a disaster occurs but it is not needed after that point. They are a store that remains open because people purchase items and they make money. They don't want Lowe's to become a glorified gemach for things like generators where you would have them hold your money as collateral while you use the item and then once you don't need it any more you can just give it back and get your collateral back. A business can't function that way.

When I called the store and asked about returning the nonfunctional generator they said that they don't take back generators. I told them that I am not returning it because I don't need it. I want to return it because is stopped working. I was told the same thing again. "We do not take back generators". I was starting to get very angry. We were talking about more than $750 here. I said that "I didn't need an expensive piece of lawn art; I need a generator that isn't defective". We went back and forth a few more times and I noticed that I was going to explode so I abruptly ended the phone call. I asked Julie if she could help me deal with it because at this point I had a very short fuse and I think that she would be able to finesse something out of them. She called Lowe's's corporate number and spoke to a very pleasant representative whose name I don't remember. She explained the situation to the representative and the representative said that I can return the generator and get my money back. She gave us her name and identification number and told us to use it if they give us a hard time. I put the enormously heavy generator in my trunk and hauled it to Lowe's. I brought it into the store and got in line in the returns department. I noticed a person ahead of me leaving from the returns desk with his head hanging low. He was mumbling under his breath, pulling a shopping cart behind him, with his generator on it as he walked out of the store because they wouldn't let him return it. I decided that I wasn't going to give up without a fight. I noticed that the people working at the returns desk kept looking at me and my generator and then looking back at their computers. After a few minutes, it was my turn. I told the woman that I wanted to return my generator because after only working for 10.5 hours it was broken. The woman politely told me that they weren't accepting any generators because it was their stores official policy. I asked her if she was sure that that was the store's policy. She told me that that's what they were instructed to say by the store's manager. I asked her to call for the stores manager to come over because I would like to deal with the boss. When he came over I told him that we had spoken to the Lowe's corporate office and that they had a different story entirely. The manager told me that he didn't know what I had heard but that the stores official policy was to not take back generators. If they started taking back tools and other equipment like generators, that people needed for a short period of time, or that they only needed to do a certain project on their home, and then return everything, the store would be losing money. I was so flustered by his response and how it was said that I didn't remember the persons' name that Julie spoke to at the corporate office so I made one up along with a contact identification number and asked him to call her because she specifically told us that we could return it for our money back because it was broken and that it didn't matter that we didn't have the original packaging. We argued back and forth a few more times and he finally asked me how I could prove to him that it's broken. I retorted by telling him that it was presently filled with 7 gallons of gasoline and it would be perfectly fine for me to take it outside and for him to try to get it started. I also said that with the gas crisis going on I could sell that 7 gallons of gas for a lot of money but all I wanted to do was return a broken generator. He stood there silently for a few minutes thinking. Finally he said that he wasn't going to go outside and try it but that he would give me store credit. He showed me on the back of the receipt where it says that if merchandise was returned to the store without its original packaging, only store credit would be given. Because I didn't have the woman's name and contact information at the corporate office I decided not to argue over getting the money back and decided to take the store credit. After all I was going to need to replace my tools and buy other things that they sell at Lowe's so it was in essentially the same thing. I walked out of the store with the gift card for over $750 and called Julie and told her what happened. She was frustrated that we didn't get the money back that we were told we would, but said that store credit would be needed anyway, so we should just leave it alone and not pursue it further. I am sure that the deciding factor for the store manager was that he wanted the 7 gallons of gas in the generator. I am sure that every drop of the seven gallons of gas made their way into the gas tank of his car later that day.

ACHIEZER MEETS SHOR YOSHUV

I knew that we were going to need a lot of boxes to facilitate the boxing up of all of our things in order to be able to remove them from the first floor but I didn't want to buy them because we hadn't gotten any money from insurance yet. I decided to utilize the roof storage bin on the roof of my car for hauling and storing them. Every day that I would go to the house I would stop off at Shor Yoshuv and go to where they throw out their boxes. I must have taken at least one hundred boxes of all different shapes and sizes and stored them in the house in preparation packing up our belongings at a later date. I had received a phone call from Achiezer letting me know that Shor Yoshuv had allowed them to use their dining room and gym to setup in. They told me that there was a food pantry that also gave people hot meals in the dining room and that the gym was being setup as a clothing gemach. I later found out that the lion's share of the food that was donated to the food pantry and the prepared foods were donated by Brach's and that it was tens of thousands of food that was donated without hesitation. The pleasant woman on the phone told me that if there was anything that we needed to please come by and grab a box or garbage bag and take what we need, no questions asked. When I went to check it out I couldn't believe my eyes. The entrance to the ezras noshim (women's entrance) was filled with children's toys, diapers, baby formula, and pretty much anything and everything that you would need to take care of a baby and it was all new and still in the original packaging. When I kept walking I went into the lunch room where I was further amazed by what I saw happening. There were tables with drinks and ready to eat hot food right next to 5 or 6 long tables covered with canned and bagged food like tuna, canned vegetables, children's cereal in individually wrapped packages as well as large cereal boxes, pasta, and the list goes on and on. I noticed at the end of the table there was a bagel station where you could take as many bagels as you want and fill them with cream cheese or tuna or white fish right next to sealed containers of milk to take home for your family. I started to tear up at the amount of chesed that was going on in my own back yard. There were people there that were not only helping others pack up boxes of food for their families but they were encouraging them to take more. I continued to walk through the area that had the vending machines that you have to pass in order to get to the gym. The vending machine area was filled with tables of hygiene products ranging from but not limited to mouth wash, tooth brushes and paste, bandages, Neosporin, and feminine care products. Finally, for the kodesh kedoshim (holy of holies) of the Achiezer gemach at Shor Yoshuv; the gym. It was filled with wall to wall racks of every kind of clothing for people of any stage of life. Everything was new with the tags still on them.

Yeshiva Shor Yoshuvs gym that was filled with clothing that was donated for those in need

I saw every article of clothing that you could imagine. Racks and racks of new winter coats, rain coats, dress coats, suits, slacks, dress shirts, dresses, skirts, Shabbos robes, T shirts, blouses, pants, under shirts, underwear, socks, shoes, tights, belts, hats, tzitzis, down blankets for people without heat, sheet sets, beckishas, and the list goes on and on in every size. I was completely blown away. While I was walking around the gym I started to tear up and get that feeling in the back of my throat that I knew I had to resist in order to avoid crying. It was not easy to hold back tears when you are constantly bearing witness to neesim vi niflaos (miracles and wonders). It was quite an emotional roller-coaster. It was one of the most beautiful yet saddening moments of my life. Feeling such overwhelmingly strong and opposing feelings simultaneously was a first for me. I was watching families that had lost everything dragging around contractor bags filled with brand new clothing. I am not sure which emotion was stronger. Was it the sadness that I felt because they had lost so much or was it the happiness I felt because so many people had come together to donate so much to be given to those who are experiencing their darkest hours. It was truly a surreal experience that evades sufficient accurate description, at least by me but I will do my best.

The next day we received a letter from FEMA informing us that we were denied. Our jaws dropped. How could we be denied? Our home was almost destroyed and we had lost so many of our things. It didn't make sense. We had seen on the news that thousands of people were getting FEMA grant checks to start to be able to rebuild their homes and lives. What made us different? Why were we being abandoned by our government and country? I can't begin to explain how angry I felt. I thought that I was going to explode. I felt like there was acid in my veins. I wanted answers and I wanted them now! We called FEMA and they told us that the letter didn't really mean that we were denied. So we asked why they used the word "denied". They didn't have a good reason but we knew that the reason was to scare and frustrate people into giving up pursuing them to get the money that they were due. The woman on the phone said that when they said that we were denied, it didn't mean that we were actually denied completely. It meant that we were denied at that time because we pay for our own home owners insurance and flood insurance policies. That doesn't make any sense to me. If the government was helping some people and not others who were devastated by the same hurricane, then that is not a level playing field. Why should we be denied any assistance merely because we paid for our own private insurance which the government forced us to have or because we are both working. I felt like we were grossly ignored by our government because we were working class people. She went on to tell us that they would send a preliminary adjuster to come to the house. Before anything would actually happen we needed to have our house inspected by the home owners and flood insurances adjusters, and find out what they were going to give us. Then we had to wait to get it and file another claim with FEMA for the difference that existed between what we lost and what we had to pay to fix the house and what we had gotten from our insurance. What a ridiculous system. Whoever thought of that should have their head examined. I had heard that FEMA was giving a little bit of money to people to help get them started with the process of rebuilding but when I inquired about it I was summarily shut down. When we got off of the phone with them we called both our flood insurance and home owners insurance companies to find out when they were going to send their adjusters so we could begin the long and arduous process of rebuilding. They said that they were swamped to the point that their staff was not sufficient. They went on to explain that they had to have adjusters sent to them from all across the country and that we would get a high priority status because of the extent of the damage and because we have children and they wanted us to be able to get our lives back together as soon as possible. Silly me, I believed them and got my hopes up. That night I received a call from a Nivneh (chesed organization) representative telling my about something called CAF 1 which stood for the Community Assistance Fund. They told me to go to an address in the Five Towns and that someone would give me a check for $2,600 which they explained was $2000 for a couple and $200 additional dollars for each child to be able to buy food and clothing and to start the rebuilding process. I just stood there speechless. I couldn't believe what I was hearing. It seemed like Hurricane Sandy was the best thing that had ever happened to me for my emuna and betachon. When I went to the address that I was told to go to, to pick up the check I saw that there was a coffee table that was completely covered by envelopes. I found it amazing that they were able to procure so much money to help the Jewish community.

OOVLECHTICHA VODERECH

The next day that I went to work I was told by my boss that she couldn't keep me at Coney anymore and that I was going to be deployed to another hospital starting the beginning of the next week. She didn't know which hospital it was going to be yet so I asked her to find out if I can make any requests. I was hoping that I would be able to be deployed to a hospital that was either in Queens or closer to my house so I wouldn't have to use as much gas or waste as much time traveling to allow me to spend more time at my house. She said that she would look into it and get back to me. The next day she found out that I was going to go to a hospital in a really nasty part of Brooklyn that shall remain nameless. For the purposes of this book, it will be called "the bad hospital". When I got home, I asked my wife if she had ever heard of the hospital, and she hadn't. Everywhere I went, I asked people if they knew anything about this hospital and no one had ever heard of it. Finally I found someone who knew about the bad hospital. All they could say was "good luck and stay safe". That was not a good sign. Now I was starting to get worried.

The day finally came that I had to report to the bad hospital. It was in a horrible neighborhood and unfortunately the hospital fit right in. The equipment was sparse and the "qualified" personnel were even rarer and more far in-between. I felt as though I was treating people in a third world country. How I missed Coney. I missed the staff, the patients, the equipment, and the level of care. One of the days that I was at the bad hospital I was taking a lunch time walk to clear my head I was on the phone with my Tanta Mindy and I heard people walking behind me and I noticed that they were getting closer which was odd because I was taking a brisk walk. The gears in my head were starting to spin faster and faster with me thinking of possible scenarios. Were they jogging slowly? Were they just walking faster than me? Or were they following me? I had no idea but I quickly got off of the phone and started to psych myself up to be able to handle what might be coming next. Just a little bit of background about me. I have received more than 10 years of martial arts training, most of it competitive. I started to plan movement patterns and look for things that I could use to my advantage as well as remembering that I always have a 4 inch hunting style gravity knife in my back pocket. Finally it began. I heard them say "nice phone and watch". Judging by what I was hearing I could tell that they were far from being upstanding citizens and that there were a few of them. I kept walking, a little bit faster now when I noticed that I saw a glass bottle about 20 feet in front of me on the sidewalk. Then I heard "hey Jew boy, I meant, nice watch and phone, give them and your wallet to me now". I quickly bent down and grabbed the bottle, broke it on a tree, took out my knife and turned around and said a bunch of things that a ben Torah shouldn't and then said, "If you want what I have come and get it" and I got into a defensive stance with my knife in 1 hand and the broken bottle in the other and I was staring them down. This wasn't the smartest thing in the world to do, but when 3 degenerates who are in their late teens to early twenties converge to mug someone I didn't think that they would stop at just taking my things. I remember saying a silent tefilah asking for protection thinking "oovlechticha voderech" (protection while traveling) and doing my best to not show any weakness, because the second I would show any hesitation I knew that the standoff would be over and a fight would ensue. I watched the whites of their eyes grow and widen as they looked at each other and weren't sure how to react. I took a step in their direction and they turned around and ran. When there was a little bit of distance between us I threw the bottle at them and turned around and started to head back to the hospital at a very brisk pace with the knife closed but in my hand. I didn't know why these things kept happening but I was happy that if they had to happen as a kaparah (a means of making up for past indiscretions) at least I had divine protection. When I went back into the bad hospital I told them what happened and I was told that it wasn't worth calling the police because nothing happened and that several months prior, one of the staff members was stabbed in the chest while taking a lunch time walk in the neighborhood in broad daylight. From then on, I would only take my lunch time walks in the courtyard of the hospital that was inside the security fence.

KIDDISH HASHEM TEXAS STYLE

I t took 3 weeks to the day to get all 3 of the adjusters to come to the house. Oddly enough, the first adjuster to come to the house was the FEMA adjuster followed by the home owners' insurance adjuster and then last but not least, the flood insurance adjuster. The flood insurance adjusters name was Mike. Mike came all the way from Texas. He was a very friendly guy. He asked us how high the water had gotten in the tidal surge from the hurricane. When I told him about the 7 ½ feet of water on the street he said that he takes his hat off for us and our troubles. While I was talking to him and showing him the damage, Julie received a call from our friends at Achiezer asking us if we needed any help. She told them that we would need some help that day and they said that they would send some volunteers over in a little while. Mike was taking measurements of the height of the mold that was growing on the walls of the first floor and then we headed toward the basement door. I told him about the need for a flashlight and that he might want to wear a facial mask because of the mold that was growing in the basement. He declined the mask and we headed down into the basement. Besides for only a few puddles in the basement it was empty, just walls and a ceiling. While we were down there it was musty, damp, and the air was being violated with a stench of sewage and mold. We didn't do any cleaning of the walls because we wanted Mike to see our basement in its full glory. I was afraid that if we did any demolition work before the adjusters got to the house that they would deny us because they wouldn't have been able to see the extent of the damage. In the 3 weeks that it took since the hurricane to get Mike to the house the bluish green mold had grown to be about ¾ inches long on the ceiling, like little putrid chandeliers. Now, Mike was from the Bible belt in Texas and kept telling us how bad he felt for us and that we by far had it worse than anyone else that he had seen for Hurricane Sandy damage. After taking pictures and taking measurements and drawing a diagram of the layout of the basement he told us that he had seen enough in the basement and said that we should demolish and remove the sheetrock in the basement as soon as possible. We stayed in the basement for a few minutes schmoozing. While we were in the basement I heard a knock on the door on the first floor and an unfamiliar voice said that they were sent here from Achiezer to help. What I didn't know was that a representative from Achiezer had called Julie right after Mike told us to rid the basement of sheetrock and they asked what kind of help we would require. Julie told them what Mike said and they came prepared for the task with hammers, contractor bags, and masks. Mike and I went upstairs to find a team of 8 different tzadeekim waiting at the door to get started. They said that they were "here to get rid of the sheetrock in the basement". I said, "come on in, you are all welcome". Mike was completely unprepared for what he was witnessing. He stood there while 8 guys whose ages ranged from teenagers to mid-fifties came in and got to work. The adults were being methodical with their hammers and crow bars and the teenagers were having a great time joking around and throwing each other into the drywall to break it down. Mike was flabbergasted. He asked me who they were and how they had gotten there so fast, he had only told us to demolish the basement less than 5 minutes prior. I told him that they were volunteers from this and other Jewish communities that have been helping out with everything and anything that they can. He couldn't believe that that many people would give up a beautiful Sunday to come and toil in mud, sewage, and mold just to help other people whom they didn't even know. He asked me how much the service costs. I kept telling him that it was free and that is what Jews do for Jews in need.

This is the job that they were able to do in our my basement in no time and with a smile on their faces

It was an immeasurable Kiddush Hashem. He said that he had been do-ing hurricane, earthquake, and other natural disaster adjustments for almost 40 years and he has never heard something so beautiful and selfless. He told us that he was at Hurricane Katrina and many other hurricanes and all he saw was people watching out for "# 1" and standing there with their hands out looking for someone to do everything for them. In the Jewish part of Far Rockaway he had seen more Jewish people helping out other people in so many ways that it makes everyone else look needy and helpless. He went on to say that we "should be proud to be a part of such a wonderful community that cares for each other as much as ours does". I was so proud of my beautiful Far Rockaway community, and still am. This time, before they left, I was able to get 1 persons name and phone number because he wanted to come back to help us in any way that we would need later on. We profusely thanked every-one for coming to help us and Mike got into it as well. He was thanking them individually by shaking their hands and patting them on the shoulders and saying what a beautiful thing they were doing and that G-D should give them more strength to continue doing such wonderful and beautiful things. This was really turning into one of the most amazing Kidush Hashems that I have ever seen. Mike went down into the basement to see how they did. It took them less than a half hour to completely empty our basement of all traces of sheetrock. They even swept up after themselves down to the last sheetrock crumbs. Mike couldn't hold back his admiration for our Jewish community. He went on and on for at least 10 minutes about how wonderful of an experience he had just witnessed and that he couldn't wait to tell everyone about it. He mentioned that because of Hurricane Sandy he had heard from most of the peoples whose homes were damaged that they planned to move away from the coast. He told me that I shouldn't ever move away from our neighborhood, even if we have to move onto a house boat, it would be worth it to stay to be a part of such a wonderful group of people. He even went as far as to ask why people in other communities weren't living by the laws of the "Bible", and that we should continue to raise our children to become a part of our community to allow it to grow and get even better. When it was time for Mike to leave, he told us to get in touch with the insurance company in a week or 2 to find out what the story was with us getting insurance money and he wished us good luck and drove off to the next Sandy victims' house. Shortly after he left we went to my parents' house and called it a day.

At this point we still had no electricity. I was too afraid to turn on the electric box in the basement because I didn't want it to catch fire and we were going to hopefully start doing work on the house. I knew that whoever was going to do any work on the house was going to need electricity to be able to get started. I called a friend of mine and asked who he would recommend that could start right away. Baruch Hashem I was recommended to an electrician who only lived a block away and who had a good reputation. I called Mittmans' electric company and he was able to replace the electric box and outlets in the basement the next day. He didn't ask for a dime of payment for 2 weeks to give us a chance to get some money to be able to afford it.

We had noticed that the children's behavior was changing from their usual pleasant demeanor at times. They were beginning to act out and we didn't know why. Julie and I sat them down and asked how they were doing. They said that they missed the house and wanted to see it for themselves. They went on to say that it was nice to see pictures but they wanted to see it for themselves and that they wanted to each pick 1 toy to bring back to my parents' house. We decided that that was a reasonable request to give them more of a sense of normalcy. After all, they wanted to make sure that their rooms on the second floor were ok and that their toys were ok. While we were driving with them in the back seats of Julie's minivan we decided to prepare them for what they were going to see to make sure that it wasn't too much of a shock for them to handle. They had only seen pictures of the damage. Pictures aren't the same thing as seeing it with your own eyes while smelling the damp musty air. When we got to the house the girls said that it didn't seem like the same house. They were told that they could only be in the house for a few minutes because of the mold in the air. I went into the house first and opened all of the windows for some extra ventilation before they came into the house. Instead of each girl picking their own toy, they decided to pick 1 communal toy to be shared. They chose a toy of Noachs Teva (ark). We told them that it was a good choice, especially given the present circumstances with the flooding of the house.

It was time to start the mold remediation process but we had no idea who to use or how to make sure that they knew what they were doing. We couldn't afford to be taken advantage of both financially and emotionally. I asked a friend in the neighborhood who I should use for mold remediation and he gave me a phone number of someone local so I had assumed that he would get back to me quickly. That was a poor assumption. It took him five days just to get back to me and when he did, he told me about things that I needed to do myself before he would even come do the house to do the work. He told me to strip the walls on the first floor twenty four inches from the floor, as well as a few other things. I thought that was ridiculous, because that was the work that I would be paying him to do. After calling him back, and leaving a message, and waiting three more days for him to get back to me, I decided to use someone else. My problem now was that I had no idea who to use. I knew that there were lots of people saying that they knew what they were doing but in actuality had little to no idea how to do mold remediation properly. I decided to walk down the block and ask a friend of mine, Alter Katz who is a contractor. I asked him if he had any idea who I should use. He told me about the mold remediation specialist that he spoke to and told me how his encounter with him went. The guy came and looked at his house and said that there was only one spot with mold on a loose piece of lumber that Alter could just pick up and throw out himself. The mold specialist then told my friend that he wasn't going to charge him for the consult because he didn't do anything. My friend then went on to tell me that this mold remediation specialist had done mold remediation for one of our other neighbors, the Rothmans, for a fraction of what other mold remediation specialist were quoting, and that he had done a good job. I immediately called Lonny Rothman and asked about his experience using this guy. Lonny told me the same thing that I had heard from Alter. Lonny said that they were courteous, professional, and did a wonderful job and that company had a cool name which made it easier to remember, The Mold Master. I immediately called The Mold Master and he picked up after two rings which was already a good sign. He came to my house later on that same day. He went on to tell me that he had worked on houses in Far Rockaway, Bayswater, Long Beach, and Bell Harbor and that I had the most damage out of anyone that he had seen. I was so proud. I guess if you are going to do something, you might as well go all the way. He went on to tell me that he would take care of everything which entailed finishing the demolition in the basement, removing the floor of the first floor, removing the sheetrock on the bottom 24 inches of the first floor, and more depending on what he finds along the way. The Mold Master, whose first name is Hemwant went on to ask what my wife and I do for a living. When I told him that I was an occupational therapist at a city hospital and my wife was a social worker at a state hospital he went on to tell me a story. He told me that a close family relative of his was in a horrific car accident and that the occupational therapist that he was treated by made a world of difference by improving the quality of his life. He then said "how can I not help two people who have both chosen professions that do nothing but help others". He then said that he would make a flexible payment plan because he knew that we were not getting insurance money right away as is unfortunately usually the case for quite a while. We shook hands and he was hired. I am very thankful that through seyata deshmiya (divine providence); Hashem put him in my life. He told me that he would be able to start working on my house in 4 days while he finished a different job. Unfortunately he also said that the first floor needed to be completely empty which meant that I had a lot of work ahead of me.

EMPTYING OUT THE HOUSE

Again, I sent out a few text messages to see if anyone was available to give me a hand. Baruch Hashem I received 4 replies. My friends Mortichia Festinger, Dave Wilzerburg, and Elisha Finnman said that they were available to come to the house on Sunday and help out. A fourth friend, Tzion Danishrod called me from New Jersey and told me that he was going to try and see if he could send some people to help as well. Now that I had a deadline it was time to find a place to store our belongings. I must have called at least 10 different places looking for either PODS (small storage trailers that you keep on your property for temporary storage) or storage rooms. I seemed to be the last one invited to the storage party because no one seemed to have anything available within a 50 mile radius. Finally, I called one last company and they told me that they had one small room left. It was a 10X 10 foot storage room on the third floor of their location in Ozone Park. I immediately agreed to take it and gave them my credit card information for the deposit. My next step was to secure a reservation with U-Haul for a box truck which bichasday Hashem (with G-D's help) wasn't a problem, I took their last one. Now we had a lot of work to do and only 4 days to do it. Every night after work Julie and I went to the house to box things up. Baruch Hashem we had some very good friends who gave up their evenings to help us. We will forever be indebted to our partner (which will be explained later on) for more reasons that I will explain later on, and to Avi Barron. They toiled for hours with us to box up our kitchen, dining room, living room, and pictures. Without their help I don't think that we would have made the deadline. I started to box up our seforim. There were a lot of them and they were very heavy and needed to go upstairs onto the second floor. Julie and I had decided to put as much as we could onto the second floor because the storage room that we had rented wasn't big enough to hold everything. We again called Achiezer to see if we could possibly get a few volunteers to help us box up the seforim and bring them upstairs. Baruch Hashem they said that they would send over a few guys in about half an hour. Later on there was a knock at the door and it was the 3 men that Achiezer had sent to help. We worked hard together to box up 4 large book cases that are 4 feet wide each and then 3 other book cases and brought it all upstairs. We lined the hallway with what looked like a cardboard box version of the old game Tetris. The Sunday before the Mold Master was scheduled to start was a very busy day in my house. Julie and I got to the house to start the cleanup effort. This consisted of filling boxes with the items that were not only out in the open, but removing things from inside furniture to make the furniture lighter and easier to move. The floor around the main entrance to the house had become so swollen due to the moisture and the expanding mold between the levels of flooring, that the door could barely be opened. Because that was the way that the furniture was going to have to come out later, the door had to be taken off of the hinges. A little bit later my friends Dave Winzerburg, Mortachie Festinger, and Elisha Finman came over to help us move everything around and clean up. About twenty minutes later I heard a knock on the door. It was a few yeshivish looking guys who I didn't recognize. One of them said that his name was Avrumi Applebaum and that he was my friend Tzion Danishrods brother in-law and that he came and brought some of his friends from his yeshiva in Brooklyn named Torah V'daas, to help. I couldn't believe how much chesed I was on the receiving end of. The yeshiva guys from Brooklyn got to work right away. They took off their hats and jackets, rolled up their sleeves and started bringing things upstairs and piling them in every available inch on top of beds, underneath beds, on top of dressers, between dressers and beds, even in bath tubs and on top of toilets. These guys would be real life Tetris world champions based on the balancing and packing excellence that they achieved. They kept asking if they could do more. It was truly beautiful and our house was coming along nicely. While they were bringing everything upstairs, my 3 friends and

I were bringing the large pieces of furniture outside and putting them in the driveway while we waited for the box truck provided by the storage facility to arrive. When we removed the area rug from the living room we found a large pile of sand that the hurricane flood waters had left behind.

The sand that was imbedded in our living room rug by Sandy's waters

Finally, the truck arrived. We carried the 4 seforim shronks, breakfront, dining room set, hutch, and sectional couch into the box truck. We strategically arranged them so that everything would fit inside to avoid damage from the trip to the storage facility. Bichasday Hashem, by the end of the day the house was finally emptied and swept clean.

The Mold Master

Monday morning at precisely 7:40 AM The Mold Master showed up at the house 20 minutes earlier than we had agreed upon. He told me that he likes to get to jobs early to prepare his staff and to make sure that they have everything that they will need for the day, before starting to work. He had a crew with him of 7 or 8 men and their equipment. Upon entering the house they immediately got to work. He walked around the house with me and pointed out what he needed to do. He told me about a few areas that he would not know the extent of the damage until he would remove the surface layers and that he would call me if anything came up. I trusted him completely and I don't say that often. He had an aura of honesty about him. He told me that at the very least he was going to have to remove the floor down to the beams, remove the Sheetrock on the bottom 24-36 inches of the first floor, remove all of the nails and screws in the basement, remove the bottom cabinets in the kitchen, remove the washer and dryer, remove the oven and stove and refrigerator and do more things than I want to list at this point. He also said that in order to do the mold abatement properly, he would have to break a hole in the foundation walls to reach the crawl space below the living room. Baruch Hashem he didn't do the work on the foundation. If he did, then he wouldn't have ever recommended our contractor, Barry. He recommended a contractor that he trusted to do the work that we were so happy with that we used him for everything else that needed to be done. He went on to tell me that doing the work in our basement would legally be a problem under the present conditions. Legally, it was considered as a "confined space" because it had a low ceiling and no windows or doors to the outside for ventilation. I told him that my plans included putting windows and a door in the basement to assist in ventilation because the basement always had a bad smell ever since we bought it just over eight years prior to the hurricane. He told me that his contractor friend was able to do that too. I met with his contractor friend Barry Mohan the next morning. He was a young guy who was partners with his brother and they also seemed trustworthy. He started the work the next day. When he made the opening in the foundation it gave them access to a space under the living room that is approximately 17 feet wide and 15 feet deep. The newly accessible area not only had a dirt floor but the dirt was piled up at least 2 feet higher than the floor in the rest of the basement. It was littered with old lumber, broken glass, and other used and damaged construction materials. I couldn't believe how much stuff was hidden behind that wall. Upon closer inspection, there was a brick column that was about 2 feet by 2 feet thick that was the lone support system for the living room and it was damaged. The living room was being supported by 1 brick that was ready to collapse.

The 1 brick that was precariously left supporting the front of our house

I went to the house daily to check the mail and to check their progress. It's not that I didn't trust that they were working, but because I am a handy person and I wanted to see how the things were being done. Each time I went unannounced and I saw that they were constantly working. This made me trust them even more and thank Hashem for sending them my way. Both Hemwant and Barry really did everything that they could to make the entire experience as pleasant as it could possibly be for us. Over the next 2 days the contractor came back and made 2 large holes in the side of the basement which used to be windows. The contractor that we bought the house from sealed all three basement windows with cinderblocks to try to get the house to stop leaking when it rained. Now that the basement was not considered a "confined space" the real work could begin. When they started to remove the floor on the first floor they couldn't believe what they were seeing. I received a call at work and Hemwant told me that underneath the floor was another floor and underneath that floor there was still another floor and underneath that floor was the original floor of the house what was put in in 1928. He was baffled by this. Seeing that each floor was put on top of the previous floor instead of removing the original floor meant that construction had never

Looking through where the first floor should have been into the basement

been done properly in the house and that previous contractors had always been cutting corners. He then told me that this was a bad sign because if they would do that, who knows what else we would encounter while parts of the house were being deconstructed. Case in point, the structurally unsound brick column in the basement that was found earlier. They left the sub floor while they removed the sheetrock and insulating materials from the bottom 30 inches of the first floor. Once that was complete, they removed the sub floor exposing the bare beams of the house.

For safety purposes they decided to create temporary walkways over the bare beams using our old doors.

It was a very unsettling feeling walking around on 2 inch wide pieces of wood that creaked when you walked on them. Not to mention that when you would look down you were looking into the basement below you so it felt like walking on a high wire at the circus without a net. One misstep and you would fall into the basement. They eventually used the doors from the coat closets, basement, and bathroom as temporary floor boards to walk on. Towards the end of the job they started to clean that new area that we opened up underneath the living room. Hemwant told me that besides not having the legal requirement of a firewall, there was no wall between us and our neighbor at all in that room and that if he didn't do the mold abatement under the front of my neighbors' house it would recontaminate our house and the mold would spread. Hemwant gave me a price for how much it would be to clean just our area and another price for how much it would be to clean both spaces. He said that it was up to me to either get my neighbor to pay for his half or I could pay for it and collect the money from my neighbor. Due to the fact that I had to be at work during the day and Hemwant was at the house during the day we decided that he would knock on my neighbors' door and talk to him about it. After a few days of not being able to get in touch with my neighbor, Hemwant decided to help us out and do it for free to help maintain my friendship with my neighbor and to save us money that we would need to pay bills and fix our house. It would have cost me about another thousand dollars. He also removed our kitchen cabinets, sinks, and counter top from the kitchen because the bottom cabinets were moldy. When he removed our kitchen cabinets we discovered what appeared to be the original wallpaper in the kitchen from the twenties. Upon further inspection, it seemed that at some point in time there was a kitchen fire in the house.

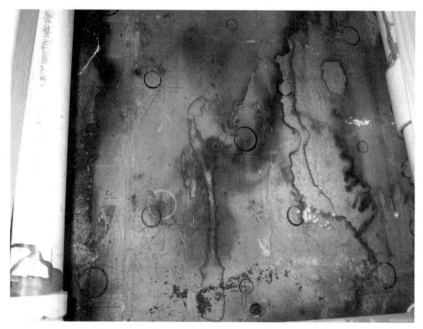

Barry had uncovered very old wallpaper in the kitchen that had evidence of a past fire in the house.

He asked me if he could take the upper cabinets and give them to a specific family in Belle Harbor that he knew that had lost everything in the storm. I happily agreed, and on the last day of the job he took the cabinets and gave them to the family. I was so happy that someone was able to benefit from our tragedy. I thanked him profusely for the opportunity to help someone else who was in a similar situation. About half way through the mold remediation process we received our home owners' insurance checks. Now we could relax a little bit and not worry about being able to pay them for the work that they had done. It took almost 2 weeks but Baruch Hashem they were finished on what happened to be a Friday. We had also received word that we were going to be receiving a $2,000 grant toward our mortgage payment from the MET council through the JCCRP. We were ecstatic about it because we needed all of the extra help that we could get.

NIVNEH AND THE COMMUNITY ASSISTANCE FUND TO THE RESCUE

O n Monday morning Barry Mohan came with his brothers to see what had to be done. Our biggest problem was that we didn't have even close to enough money to pay him yet. We were able to give him $5,000 which was all that we had to get him started. He said that that would be enough to purchase a small amount of the materials, probably enough to keep them working for about 4 days. He expected the job to take 3-4 weeks and cost just under $40,000. He said that normally he would need a third to get started to buy the materials that he needed but in our case he would work with us, as far as a payment schedule was concerned, to help us out. The 2nd payment would be due one and a half weeks later and the final payment would be due upon the completion of his work. We told him that as long as we get the money from the insurance company within that time frame we would be happy to keep to that schedule. He then told us that if we don't get all of the money by then, he would give us a one month extension on the final payment but would appreciate it if we would try to find the money from somewhere if possible. I told him that I would get in touch with him either later on that day or the next day and I went back to my parents' house.

When I got to our house I broke down. I told Julie that they need at least $10,000 quickly in order to have them continue to work for more than 4 days. If we don't get that $10,000 quickly, they will leave us and go to another job because we don't have the money to keep them working on ours.

That was $10,000 that we didn't have. I told her that I felt like I was drowning. I felt like no matter how hard I tried to swim and get things done I kept sinking into despair. The next day I received a call from a friend of ours. She told me about an organization called Nivneh that was trying to help people who were affected by hurricane Sandy by distributing funds from another organization of tzadeekim called the Community Assistance Fund (CAF) that had raised the money. She also told me that she would like to be our liaison to remove some of the burden from my shoulders. I felt so touched that our friend who was busy with children, working, constantly being involved with chesed projects, and being the president of Nishay Shor Yoshuv, was willing to make time in her busy life to help us make ours more bearable. What an incredible human being and friend. She told us that it was called the "partner program". I would love to put her name all over this book to acknowledge what she has done for us but she asked her Rav and he said that it would be better to not have her name in the book for sneus (modesty) purposes. I will respect her wishes and use the word "partner" in lieu of her name. Over the next few months we were constantly receiving phone calls, text messages and e-mails from our guardian angel about different opportunities for us as they became available. I will explain that more as the instances occurred during the following months later on in the story. She told me to call Yitzie Halpern and to explain the situation to him and that he would be our liaison between us and the powers that be who make the decisions about who to give and how much to give each person, depending on their specific situation. To make a long story short, he was able to hand me a $10,000 check from the Community Assistance Fund to give to the contractor to get him started and to keep him working for about a week and a half. It was a surreal experience. I couldn't believe that I was holding a $10,000 present that would make fixing our home possible. It was as if I had a car that I couldn't drive and someone just handed me the keys as a present. We shook hands and he wished me hatzlocha (success) and told me that I should call him if I have any further questions and problems. Later on that day I handed the contractor, Barry, the check and he told me that he would go to Home Depot and buy the materials that he needed and get started on our house the next morning. Some of the things that we discussed doing to the house were removing and replacing some of the damaged floor support beams, changing the dimensions of the kitchen to make it larger, putting windows and a door in the basement for ventilation and ease of access, installing the floors, installing the bathroom, painting the first floor, fixing leaks here and there, digging down in that new area below the living room, and numerous other things that were both planned and unexpectedly came up. There were many more things that he had to do but I will not go into all of them. It was a tall order and he was going to be very busy for a while. After the first week and a half of working we already saw a huge difference in the house. Unfortunately it was time to give him the second installment but we didn't have the money in our possession yet. Earlier, my father in-law had told us that if we need financial help he would be happy to loan us whatever we need until we can pay him back interest free. Baruch Hashem we had an alternative avenue for temporary funding to utilize. We called him and Baruch Hashem he said that Julie could come and pick up the check the next day. We gave the check to Barry and construction kept going as scheduled without losing any momentum.

It was already the dead of winter and Barry told me that it was getting to be very cold in the house. Their only source of heat was 2 small plug-in electric heaters. It was time to call someone about replacing the boiler and hot water heater and trying to borrow the money to pay for it if need be. I knew just the tzadik to call. I called Shikey Munchik. I chose to call him because he has a history of doing chesed for us. During Hurricane Irene our basement flooded and rendered our hot water heater inoperable. I asked around for names and numbers of who to call and his name kept coming up. With a reputation like that how could we use someone else? When he came to the house he said that it would be best to replace it. When I told him that we couldn't afford to replace it because I was currently unemployed he went right to work trying to salvage the existing hot water heater. He kept working on the hot water heater until he found a way to jerry rig it to make it work. When I asked him how much I owe him for the house call and the repairs he was a tzadik gomure and told me that "it was on the house" and he gave me a bracha of hatzlocha and wouldn't take any money. I gave him a bracha of hatzlocha and thanked him profusely and he said that the thanks were not necessary. That is why I decided to call him again. He sent his partner

Bentzion to evaluate the situation and see what could be done. He told me that to replace what we originally had would be about $6,000 but that if we wanted to replace what we had he was not going to take the job. He went on to explain to me how the hot water heater and boiler systems weren't legally installed to the codes of safety because of the low ceiling height in the basement. Because he was honest enough to be willing to walk away from a job because of safety concerns I was even more positive that he was the person that I wanted to do the job. He told me about a different kind of system that would work well for us but it was more expensive, he told me that it was a combination system that would heat the house and heat the hot water with a greater level of efficiency but that it would be more than $9,000 to purchase and install. He went on to tell me about another version of the system that would be much more efficient but that it would cost $12,500. I called Julie and explained our options and we decided to go with the more expensive model because it would raise the efficiency of the system from about 84% up to 95%. We also told him that we wanted the house to be turned into 2 zones instead of one because the old thermostat was on the first floor and the first floor had better insulation than the second floor. The combination of the location of the existing thermostat and poor insulation on the second floor caused the first floor to always be comfortable and the second floor to always be cold unless the windows on the first floor were kept open. It was always an annoying and frustrating task to wake up in the middle of the night and be cold and have to go down stairs and open the windows to get the heat to be turned on on the second floor to heat up our bedrooms. He told me that he would front us the money for the unit until we had the money to pay him. While I am writing this I feel the same sentiment that I did while it was happening. I told him how much I appreciated what he was doing for us.

I called our partner and asked about what she had previously told us about which was known as CAF 3. We were told that we were approved for another $10,000 in assistance through CAF 3. I was told that all I had to do was to get a bill that explained the necessity for what was needed and bring it to a man in Far Rockaway. Unfortunately I was unable to drop it off because it was during working hours so Bubbs said that she would be our sheliach (messenger). After Bubbs was given the check and got back to her car she immediately called me. When my phone rang I saw that it was Bubbs and when I picked up I asked her how it went. I could hear that she was crying on the other end of the phone but they weren't tears of sorrow, they were tears of joy and awe. She told me that she went to the house and sat in their living room while the tzadik in charge of dispensing the CAF chesed checks was busy talking to a different Sandy victim who needed help. When that person left, Bubbs was asked to go into his study. Bubbs said that she sat there explaining our situation to him and about how much money the new system costs and she then handed him the bill with the justification letter and he read it in front of her silently. While he was reading it she noticed a pile of envelopes on his desk that had people's names on them as well a number that corresponded to the order in which they applied for CAF 3. The man finished reading the justification letter/bill and took out his checkbook and wrote out a check for $10,000 and handed it to Bubbs and gave us many brachos. My mother said that she just sat there with the check in her hands and didn't know what to do. She had never seen such chesed first hand. She said that her hand was quivering while holding the check and she noticed that our check was number 179. That means that they have helped at least that many families before us and who knows how many families were helped after us. She thanked him profusely and walked out toward her car and just sat in the car, frozen and crying. That was when she called me. She went on to emphatically say "Jesse, you better know that Hashem loves you and your family and that he is taking care of you! You better appreciate how much He loves you!" It was a sizable infusion of positive mussar that will stay with me. In the coming months when I would get depressed at times, that speech that she gave me would help to lift my spirits and strengthen my emuna. Baruch Hashem, a few days later Bensi (short for Bentzion) came with his crew and I gave him the check and he gave us the gift of heat and hot water. It's a funny thing that most people never have to even entertain as a thought. How many people actually appreciate the simple fact that when you flip a light switch it actually goes on? How many people actually appreciate the simple fact that you can walk into your own home and just stand on the floor without looking down to make sure that you don't fall into the basement between the beams? I was beginning to have a tremendous appreciation for the "little things" in life. Bensi started the job on a Friday and finished the job on Sunday. That Monday, I got a call from Barry thanking us for the heat in the house. He said that this was the first time that they weren't able to see their own breath inside the house. Barry told me that they were going to start to dig down in that new area under the living room which we wanted to use as an exercise room/guest room. From now on I will refer to it as "the new room". He had to remove about 5 feet of dirt, silt, and debris before he could pour the concrete. When they went into the new room to make sure that it was structurally stable they noticed that the support beam between my neighbor and myself was totally unsupported and sagging. That was a big problem. Barry told us that all of the structural damage between the sagging beam and the poorly fabricated brick beam were not solely caused by the Hurricane. He told us that if the hurricane hadn't come and alerted us to the hidden damage that the house would most likely have collapsed without warning in less than a year. I couldn't believe that Hashem used the hurricane to destroy our home to save our lives. Seyata deshmaya is a beautiful thing. We decided that we were going to build a cinderblock wall underneath the sagging beam to not only separate our new room from my neighbor's house but it would also support the sagging beam and function as the firewall that the house was missing as well. Barry said that he had no experience digging down several feet below the water table in such a damp area and putting a floor down and making a room like that. He told me that he would do his best but that he didn't know if it would work and that it might flood. I told him to go ahead and try anyway.

Just an interesting side note; one of the days that I was at our house I received a call from my friend Ross. The same Ross that is a member of Hatzala who came to my parents' house to take Julie to the hospital earlier. He is one of the many police officers who were reassigned in and around the Jewish section of Far Rockaway to increase the police presence to help avoid looting and violence in the less desirable part of the neighborhood as well as keeping it from spilling into our area. He asked if I was at the house and I told him that I was. He asked me if I have an Artscroll gemara Berachos volume 2? I told him that I had one and that it was not damaged by the storm. He told me where he was stationed and asked if I could bring it to him because he was not allowed to leave his post for personal reasons and he had forgotten his at his apartment in Queens. I said "sure, it would be my pleasure" and then he told me where he was located. He was stationed in the middle of a large intersection that was only about 10 blocks away. I told him that I would be there in a few minutes. I took the gemara into my car and drove over there. Once I saw where he was I pulled up alongside him and made the gemara handoff. About a month later he made a siyum on Berachos.

We received a phone call from our partner to tell us that Nivneh had vouchers to assist us in buying new appliances for the house from a store in Brooklyn called The Buzz. We were elated. We went to pick them up and then headed to Brooklyn. The vouchers amounts added up to about $1,700. We ordered the first new appliances for the house; a washer and dryer. They were delivered through one of the large holes that we had made in the basement wall which would later become a small door. Later on we purchased our oven from them as well. We bought the rest of the appliances at PC Richard and Sons for several reasons. Julie's aunt Lidia gave us a generous check

The broken sewage line

to assist us with the purchase. She said that instead of donating the money to the Red Cross and having the money go to people that she didn't know she would rather give it to someone that was affected by the storm that she not only knows, but that is related to her. Julie's grandmother Oomie also gave us a generous gift which really helped us with the purchase of our kitchen appliances. On top of the other reasons that brought us to P.C. Richards was that Julie was friends with the managers wife so he gave us all of the discounts that he could which really made a huge difference in the financial burden.

I received a phone call from Barry. He didn't sound very happy. He said that he has some bad news for us. He told me that while they were removing the silt, dirt, sand, and debris from the new room in the basement they noticed a big problem that he didn't think that he could fix.

Our water main and sewage line were broken. He said that he definitely couldn't fix the sewage line because it was made of clay but that he would attempt to repair the water main. He did mention that the success of the repair of the water main wouldn't be a permanent solution and might not even be a good temporary one. He said that he would do his best, especially because he knows how much it costs to replace a water main and sewage line. I received another call from him the next day. Unfortunately, the water main sprung another leak and was flooding the new room and the rest of the basement. He told us that we had to get them fixed and fixed on a professional level from someone who specializes in water mains and sewage lines. I had no idea who to call for water main and sewage line repairs, but I have a neighbor who used a company named Liberty Sewage and Water and was very happy with the job. I called Liberty Sewage as well as 2 other large companies to get price quotes. Liberty quoted me a price of $10,000 and the other 2 gave me quotes of $16,000 and $22,000. This is not the kind of thing that you want to necessarily choose the cheapest option but my friend was happy with the job that they did and they were given very high scores from past clients that I looked up online. I called them and told them what I needed fixed and they said that they could come and start the job in a week and a half. I said yes and now our largest presenting problem was that we needed $10,000 dollars that we didn't have to appear from somewhere and in a hurry. A few weeks prior to this a person in our extended family, who does not want any recognition for what they did, called us and told us that if we need any financial help, we should just call them and they would lend it to us without interest for as long as we need. I decided to call them and explain our present situation and humbly ask for the $10,000 that was needed to pay for the repairs. He was a tzadik. He made me feel like this money was burning a hole in his pocket and that I was doing him a favor by "allowing" him to lend it to me. He made a very unpleasant and uncomfortable experience not only pleasant but he built up our self-esteem at the same time by not only empathizing with us, but telling us how impressed he was with how we were handling the situation. For that I will always be grateful. We were told that we would have the money and it would clear in 1 week. Fortunately and unfortunately at the same time, I had received a phone call from Liberty. They said that they could come earlier but that they would still need to be paid at the time of the job being done. That wasn't enough time for us to get his check and for it to clear. We didn't know what to do. After much deliberation we formulated a plan. We would try to borrow the money from my parents and in-laws and use some of our money to pay Liberty Sewage. We could not afford to empty our bank account and have no money to spare because we needed to have something in our bank account to be able to pay bills. When the other check for $10,000 clears we would use it to be able to pay back my parents and in-laws. We only had about $4,000 left in our bank account. We asked my in-laws if we could borrow $5,000 which they gladly said yes to. We then asked my parents if we could borrow $3,000 and they were happy to say yes. Baruch Hashem we were able to pay for the sewage line and water main to be replaced. A few days later when the other check cleared we were able to use that money to pay our parents back. I love it when a plan comes together.

I had received a phone call out of the blue from one of the most influential people in this stage my life, Rabbi Tzvi Yaakov Stein. Let me backtrack a little bit. Before Rabbi Stein came into my life I wasn't really learning at all but I was going through the day to day motions. It had been years since I was learning with a set sayder (learning schedule), let alone anything other than seforim that were translated into English. I have had random sparks if inspiration from time to time where I would pick up a sefer and want to start a seder but they always seemed to fizzle rather quickly. I was once at the Shabbos table of a friend of mine and he gave a great divar Torah. He spoke about inspiration. I believe that he said that it was told over by the Rambam. He said that inspiration is compared to lightning and that we are walking in a dark forest at night during a thunder storm and can't see where we are going but we are trying to get to our destination. We have a place in mind that we would like to travel to but at night every direction looks the same in an unfamiliar forest. We try to get to our target but in the dark without any light each tree looks like the next and you end up going around in circles. The smart thing to do is to wait for the lightning and to move toward your destination as soon as the sky lights up and your path is visible and clear. The Rambam is saying that as soon as inspiration strikes you must act on it. As soon as you have that moment of clarity if you don't do something then and there then it is lost forever. If lightning strikes and you are in those dark woods of stagnation and you don't act on those moments of clarity then you will never get out of the woods. Rabbi Stein has been my lightning. Ever since he was introduced to me, I and many other people just gravitate toward him as if he has a gravity of kedusha and understanding that he is infused with. His personality is magnetic and his love of yiddishkite is infectious. For over a year now, I have been proud to be a member of a fantastic group of guys who learn with him at least 3 times a week. I have even taken upon myself to learn daf yomi which if you would have told me that I would have now undertaken 6 months ago I would have laughed at you. His shiurim have become so important to us that many of them have been recorded and put online in order to listen to them at our leisure. We even have a member of the shiur who moved to Arizona but is able to attend our Monday night shiur in Bays Water through Skype on my cellphone. He can even be an active participant in the shiur through the cell phones speakerphone. Rabbi Stein has become one of the most important and influential people in my life, even though if asked, he would shrug it off and say that I was crazy. Enough with the background information and back to the story line. It was just a normal day, I had come back to my parents' house after work and I had just sat down on the couch and put my feet up when my cell phone rang. The caller ID said that it was Rabbi Stein. I picked up and asked if everything was alright and what I could do for him. He told me that that was not the reason why he was calling me. I said that I was doing well and I mentioned about going to davening and being diligent with my daf yomi learning. He stopped me and said that that wasn't what he was asking. He said that he didn't want to make sure that I was going to daven or learning or even being a good Jew. He wanted to know how I was handling everything emotionally, as a person. It was one of the most touching phone calls I have ever received. There was a lot of musar packed into that concept as well. I am not my learning and my davening. Yes, they are a part of me but I am the person who is choosing to do or not to do them. Even though he was seeing me on a regular basis at our Monday night shiurim which I was now driving in for from Fresh Meadows Queens. He didn't want to ask me in front of everyone else where I might feel like I had to puff out my chest and say that I was being a man and that I was toughing it out. He wanted to ask me in a more intimate setting to see how I was actually doing. I told him that we were doing alright most of the time but that we hit our walls along the way. Baruch Hashem we were receiving tremendous amounts of support and chesed which made everything much easier to deal with. As rough as things got we were always able to reflect upon the help that we had received. I went on to explain how our lives seemed to be one big game of Whack a Mole. For those who aren't familiar with Whack a Mole, it is a carnival game where there are mechanical moles that pop up out of multiple holes in a table and you are given a hammer and told to hit them when they pop out of the holes which knocks them back into the table. Every time you hit one and they go back inside another one or two pup up in different places which you then have to hit and the cycle continues until the game is over. I told him that I can't wait for the game to be over and for our normal lives to begin again. He gave me some words of chizuk and gave us berachos and told us that if we ever want to come back to far rockaway for Shabbos we were welcome and that his home and cellphone were always open to us. I thanked him and ended the phone call. He is involved in so many people's lives but he took time out of his busy schedule to make time for me. I felt honored. That phone call meant a lot to Julie and myself and helped us get through the darker times that we had to come kind of like a "get out of depression free" card.

We had gotten another email from our Nivneh partner on Monday telling us about a family in Lawrence that wants to give a swing set away and she thought of us because our old swing set was made of metal and was now rusting away in the back yard. Once I saw the E-mail I showed the picture to Julie and we decided to go for it if it was still available. I texted our partner and said that we would love to be the recipients of the swing set. Baruch Hashem, she said yes and that we have the rights to it but that we had to remove it from the property as soon as possible. She gave me their name and phone number. I called them and asked if I could come and take it Sunday morning. They said that that would be fine. I quickly sent out another set of chesed text messages to my friends asking if anyone was available to help me out. Baruch Hashem I got several friends who said that they were available to help. This time it would be Papa, Eran Saidi, Elisha Finman, and Simcha Wertzel. When that Sunday morning came, I got to their house and let them know that I was the one that they had spoken to about taking the swing set. I didn't want them to be nervous about a U-Haul in their driveway and people who they didn't know taking things out of their yard. The swing set was in amazing condition. They had taken very good condition of it over the years by having it repainted with water proof paint every year. We quickly dismantled the swing set and took it to my back yard in 2 trips with the U-Haul. Before we left their house for the 2nd and final trip I thanked them again for their generosity. They told me that the swing set was meant to have 3 swings but that the swings themselves were in bad shape and that we should buy 3 new swings and bring then the receipts and that they would pay for them. I couldn't believe that they were so unbelievably generous. I graciously thanked them for what they had given and offered us, and told them that Baruch Hashem, our swings had survived and that we were going to use them and didn't need 3 new swings. After getting back to my backyard, before putting the swing set together we first had to remove the old one. I figured that I would have to fight with the swing set to take it apart because it was made out of metal, held together by nuts and bolts, was now covered with rust, and also because I would have to remove the poles that were cemented into the ground. The night before, I had gone to the house and sprayed every nut, bolt, and metal seam with a rust removing spray that was used by automotive mechanics. It contains enzymes that eat away at rust to hopefully, make the dismantling of the swing set easier to accomplish. That spray worked wonderfully. Each nut and bolt and metal joining seam came apart as if it was a new swing set that I was disassembling. When it was time to remove the swing set from the ground I noticed the ground in my back yard was so waterlogged and loose that I was able to pull the old swing sets poles which were cemented in to the ground out of the ground with almost no effort at all. Once the old swing set was dismantled and removed from the area we got to work on the new swing set. We were putting the newly acquired swing set back together at a breakneck pace in order to have it finished before Julie and Bubbs got to the house with the kids. Baruch Hashem we finished it about 2 minutes before they arrived. The kids were astonished. They said that it was much better than the old swing set and immediately began to climb on it and discover what it had to offer.

Within 5 seconds of the kids seeing the new swing set, they were hard at play

After we had finished playing, and I returned the U-Haul we went to the family that had graciously donated the swing set and thanked them personally, this time with the children present. At this point we had a huge pile of debris in the front of our yard. According to the NYC policy, we were supposed to be able to call 311 and report debris on private property and they were supposed to come and pick it up. Unfortunately the reality was far from that. No matter how many times I called 311 and asked them to come and remove it they never came. I was given a price quote of how much it would be to pay to have it hauled away. I was told that it would be at least two thousand dollars which I didn't have to spare.

Finally I had decided to try another avenue to try to avoid the extra expense. I had heard about organizations that were funded by the Robin Hood Foundation that would have volunteers come to bag up and remove debris from the storm and from home repairs. I called them and explained our situation and within 3 days, all of the debris was gone, Baruch Hashem.

All of this disappeared in one day

Just another side note. During Chanukah we had received a sizable package from Nivneh. It was filled with wrapped gifts for the girls. They really did a great job of supporting and protecting the simchas ha chag of Channuka for us. On the second night of Channuka, my oldest daughter, Devorah Nechama had received $1 as a gift. She said that she didn't want to keep it for herself. She wanted to give it to someone that needed money to help with the repairs to their house from Hurricane Sandy damage. She asked if we know any Rabbis that could use it. We mentioned Rabbi Freed and his family, who we have known for more than 10 years and regularly attend Shabbos meals. She was so excited that her dollar would go to a Rabbi that we know and love. She asked for an envelope and she decorated it and wrote a message on it and put the dollar bill inside.

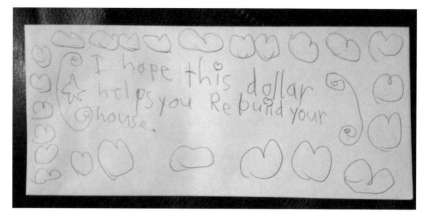

The envelope that contained Devora Nechamas $1 gift for the Freed family

She brought it to school the next day and gave it to Rebbitzin Freed who is a teacher in her school. When Devora Nechama came home after school that day she was so happy. She told us all about how she gave it to Rebbitzin Freed and how she thanked her and about how great it felt to help someone in need. Who knows, maybe when she grows up she will become a chesed guru like our Nivneh partner. We can only hope.

We decided that since we were the recipients of so much bracha, nisim, and seyata deshmaya that we wanted to show *hakaras ha tov* to the Rebone Shel Olam for protecting us from dangers that were obvious and hidden. We also wanted to thank our parents and their community for not only accepting us, but for offering their assistance. We decided to sponsor a kiddish at my parents' shul, Ohr Moshe. The people in the Ohr Moshe community were offering us clothing and giving us chizuk in our time of need. Some of the people in the community even had us over for Shabbos meals and called us to make Shabbos afternoon play dates with our children to bring their lives some semblance of normalcy.

Julie received a phone call from the Rosh Yeshiva of Shor Yoshuvs Rebetzin, Rebetzin Jaeger. She spent almost an hour giving Julie chizuk and comfort. Rebetzin Jaeger also made a request. She wanted us to come as a family to their home to schmooze and because the Rosh Yeshiva and the Rebetzin were discussing our situation and wanted to give Julie a matana (gift). After getting off the phone with Rebetzin Jaeger, Julie began to cry. When I inquired why she was crying, she told me about the conversation that she had with Rebetzin Jaeger. She said that the phone call made her feel like royalty. Julie said "out of the hundreds of people in the community, who were we to have the Rosh Yeshiva and Rebetzin worry about us? There are hundreds of people who daven at Shor Yoshuv every week, and we were singled out". She said that she was star struck and couldn't believe that they were not only concerned with our wellbeing but that we were going to go to their house. We went to the Rosh Yeshiva and Rebetzins home that Sunday. Throughout the entire car ride Julie kept saying how nervous she was and honored at the same time. When we got to their house we rang the doorbell and Julie took a deep calming breath. Rebetzin Jaeger opened the door and invited us in. Not even 2 seconds after the door closed behind us the Rebbitzin gave Julie a big hug and whispered something in her ear that I couldn't hear. She then bent over and started to talk to our girls. She was asking them how they were and their names and how old they were. They were shy but still answered her with some parental prodding. Rebetzin Jaeger told us that the Rosh Yeshiva apologized for not being able to be there but he was at the Yeshiva and couldn't leave. We were invited to come into the kitchen and she asked us if we wanted something to drink and the girls if they would like some candy and cookies. The girls were so excited to get candy from Rebetzin Jaeger. The Rebetzin was asking us how we were coping with our situation and gave us words of much needed chizuk and brachos. It meant a lot to all of us. We then went to the living room and all sat down on the couch and continued to schmooze with Rebetzin Jaeger. We were enamored by the Rebetzins warmth, depth of caring, and eloquent speech. We were there for about an hour but it seemed like a minute. Towards the end of our visit, Rebetzin Jaeger said that she had a matana for Julie from her and the Rosh Yeshiva. She handed Julie an envelope with a check in it and said that the money wasn't for paying bills or to go to the house. She said that it was specifically to be used for something for Julie; something that she normally wouldn't do for herself. She went on to say that Julie deserved it because of the wonderful job that she was doing to hold us together and keeping us positive. We thanked her profusely and she gave Julie another big hug and gave us more chizuk and more brachos before we left her home. While we walked back to the car Julie started to cry again, and talk about how wonderful the Rosh Yeshiva and Rebetzin are and what a huge impact they have made on her. She slowly opened the envelop and saw that it had a check in it. Julie said that she didn't want to cash it. She wanted to keep it in a frame. She ended up taking a picture of it and depositing it, even though she would rather have kept it as a keepsake.

We were receiving constant emails and text messages from our partner about different opportunities for not only financial assistance but for house hold items that people were donating for Sandy victims. We were offered everything from a marble dining room table; tread mills, kitchen appliances, china, glass ware, silver ware, bedroom furniture, clothing, seforim, cleaning services, children's toys, and much much more. Since the hurricane we must have received, without exaggeration, at least 150 text messages, emails, and phone calls about different people who wanted to donate things to Sandy victims. She even told us about different stores that were offering discounts on clothing, furniture, and children's toys for Hurricane Sandy victims. Some of the emails and texts were about grants that we could apply for and left over food from different events that she was a part of. So far to date we have received school supplies, a children's kitchen set, a plata, a hot water urn, bicycle, swing set, and the list goes on and on. She also told us about a Red Cross grant that we could apply for for assistance with paying for home repairs, which we quickly applied for. We will forever be indebted to her for the help and for the peace of mind that she has provided us with. Later on we found out that we weren't the only family that she was helping. She was a partner to three other families. I was astounded by her dedication and boundless chesed even more when I heard that.

A few days later our partner called us again and asked us if we would meet her at the Nivneh warehouse. She said that it was filled with household items and that we should meet her there to see what we need. She told us where it was on the Yeshiva Darchay Torahs grounds and we met her there. We couldn't believe what we were looking at; it was an overwhelming sight to behold.

A portion of the Nivneh warehouse

With all of the amazing things that we have seen it was incredible that we could still be amazed and impressed with each new explosion of chesed that we saw. It was amazing to see the chesed that had been focused on our community that came from within and from across the country. It was a large room filled with everything that we could possibly need and more. There were sections for baby food, kitchen goods, school supplies, non-perishable food, toys, kitchen appliances, bedding, and the list is practically endless. After several trips to the car and back we had amassed quite a few household items that we needed. We received some serving pieces, some toys for the kids, snacks for the kids, a food processor, and more. We were very grateful for everything that we were given. Just when we didn't think that it was possible to fall more deeply in love with our community, our feelings still were able to grow in intensity and depth. Later on I found out that Nivneh was created because of Hurricane Sandy. It was not a pre-existing chesed organization. Ettie Schoor is a woman who lives in the neighborhood who owns a company called Prism Consultants that specializes on workers compensation insurance and risk management for the health care industry. She took many of her resources and staff and created Nivneh and had her staff using their specific skill customer service to help the community. She had over 600 volunteers helping them as well. She had teams in Atlanta, Montreal, Toronto, Lakewood, Passaic, Cleveland, Monsey, Bayswater, Far Rockaway, Lawrence, Woodmere, Cedarhurst, and Eretz Yisroel all playing roles in this tremendous chesed project. It really bogles the mind what a Yid will do for other Yiden.

The house was coming along nicely. We decided to take a family trip to see how the progress was going. When we opened the door I noticed that the sub floor was installed, but I didn't tell the kids or Julie who were behind me on the stairs. I walked in and waited to see and hear their reactions.

The girls playing on the plywood floor of the house, excited that they had any floor to stand on

They were so excited. The kids were running around the house while Julie just cried with a huge smile on her face. We were all so excited to see that our house was well on its way to becoming a home. From then on, every time we went back to the house there were even more drastic changes. The next time we went back to the house the floors were being installed and the walls were painted. Finally, neesim vi niflaos, on the next trip to the house we could say that the walls and floors were done.

The new dining room in our practically new home

It was absolutely beautiful. We no longer had a house. It was now a home. Because of what we had just went through, and with all that we had seen, we decided that a normal mezuzah would not be sufficient. Normal mezuzas are for normal houses. This was no ordinary home any more. It was rebuilt by Siyata deshmaya by the yad of Hashem. We decided that it would only be fitting to have the mezuzah placed inside of the door post instead of upon it. It is a constant reminder that Hashem rebuilt this home for us using the various tools at his disposal.

The house that we bought had a mezuza afixed to the doorpost. This house was rebuilt for us using open miracles so we decided to have the mezuza put inside of the doorpost to remind us of the nisim that we witnessed.

We still needed a kitchen, new windows, alarm replaced, cement staircase demolished and rebuilt out of synthetic deck material, new window cut out of the basement wall, and for the back yard to be redone because of all of the debris that was imbedded in the ground. We didn't care about all of the things that lay ahead. We were reveling in the moment. We had a home. Now we had to figure out how to pay the contractor the final lump sum of money that we owed him. We didn't want to string him along any longer than was necessary. We kept calling the flood insurance company to try to speed up the process of receiving the final check in order to make that final payment to Barry. When we were starting to talk about when to move back into the house my parents said that we were welcome to stay longer in order to give us more time to setup and organize the house. Even though that would have made more sense on paper, we were so excited to get back into our home that it wasn't an option. We thanked them for the offer but told them that we would have to respectfully decline. All sights were aimed at getting back into our home as soon as possible. Our main target was to be home before Purim. Finally, we received the insurance check in the mail and were able to give Barry the final payment to give us some semblance of closure for the time being, until he would come back to help us with some odds and ends.

Now we needed a kitchen. We decided to use a friend of ours, Noftolie Landow. I know him from Shor Yoshuv and he is also an Ohr Dovid alumni. He came and measured and we chose everything from the cabinets to the style of sink to the countertops and back splash. The way that the scheduling worked out, we were only going to live in the house for a few days without a kitchen. We had decided to move back into our home the Sunday before Purim. I sent out my usual text messages looking for some help and I reserved a U-Haul.

Finally, the day came that I was going to get our furniture out of the storage facility as well as out of my friends' garages. My friends Mordachie Festinger, Elisha Finnman, and David Winzelberg said that they would come and help me again. After I picked up the U-Haul we first went to the storage place and emptied it.

After we brought all of the furniture into the house and put it where it was supposed to go, we began to remove all of the contents that were stored on the second floor and brought them downstairs. By the time we were finished with that we were exhausted. We took a break and then went to Danielle and Noftoly Sudwertzes home. They graciously let us store some of our

Our storage unit with the large pieces of furniture from the first floor of out house.

furniture in their garage for the almost 4 months since the hurricane ravaged our home. They mentioned that they had a hutch with glass doors that an old tenant of theirs had left behind because it was unwanted. We were elated because we were going to buy a new hutch and now we didn't have to. Unfortunately we had forgotten the furniture that we had left across the street in Mordachies' garage and headed back to my house and unloaded the truck again. Everyone had to leave accept for Dave. I thanked them for their help and Dave asked if there was anything else that he could help me with. He insisted. So we got to work and brought more things down from upstairs. We were both exhausted, I thanked him and he went home and I went to return the U-Haul. Then I went back to my parents' house and was so tired that I fell asleep with my clothing on. Julie had to wake me up so that I would take off my filthy clothing and get changed for bed.

THE PLAGUE

The next Shabbos I started to have a strong and persistent cough. No matter what I did, it wouldn't even slow down. It got to the point that I wasn't able to talk without coughing to the extent that I would either throw up or feel like my chest was going to explode. Luckily Bubbs has a friend that it a pulmonologist, and a good one. Dr. Donath was a tzazik. He had me come to his house motzi Shabbos to see how I was and to see if it warranted further examination. He was not happy with that he heard in my chest and told me to come to his office the following day. He opened his office just for me and had me come in to see if he could diagnose and hopefully treat whatever was going on inside of my lungs. He had me breath into a tube with as much force as I could muster to check how much air my lungs could expel. He also took blood work and a painful sinus swab. He was not happy with what he saw. My tidal volume, which is the amount of air that you can expel with a forced breath, was so low because my lungs were not only inflamed, but because I couldn't even complete the test. I would start to cough relentlessly in the middle of the test. He put me on strong antibiotics with a prolonged treatment period, an inhaler, and a sinus rinse with a daily regimen. I was told that I had to at least wait for the results from the testing to come back from the lab before I could go back to work. He also had me get a chest x-ray. It happens to be that that Monday was the first day that I had to miss work and call out sick. My coughing was so bad that I had trouble eating. Because talking would immediately bring on a barrage of coughing, I relied upon the Google translate application on my cell phone. Google translate is usually used to translate between 2 different languages. I set it to translate from English to English. I would type what I want to say and press the speaker button and it would say what I typed out in a loud robotic voice. It was comical at times, but unfortunately a necessary tool in order to communicate. Besides for the coughing, vomiting, and pain in my chest, head, and back, the worst part was that I couldn't even hug my family since we didn't know what I had. A few days later received a call from Dr. Donath. I was told that due to my prolonged exposure to the mold and other toxins in my basement I had contracted a bacterial infection in my lungs and sinuses. Fortunately the course of treatment was the same as I had already been given so I had a head start, but unfortunately I had to continue to miss work and use my sick time, but Baruch Hashem, I had the time to use. I ended up being out for that entire week and the following Monday. Unfortunately I was home sick for all that time, but looking on the bright side, that week that I was home sick was my last week at the bad hospital. Before reporting to Coney I had to go back to Dr. Donath and not only be evaluated to see if it was safe for me to go back to work, but I needed a doctor's note to hand to the hospital that explained my absence and that explained that I was cleared for duty in a hospital. When I went to Dr. Donaths office, the difference was like night and day. I only coughed 2 or three times during the entire examination which took about 30 minutes. I felt like a new man. About 1 week after I started to work back at Coney I was informed that the bad hospital had decided to clean house. They fired not only the head of the occupational therapy department but they fired the overwhelming majority of the supervisors and staff, probably for gross incompetence. I think that the administration had finally seen the problems that I had noticed from the first day that I was deployed there and decided that it cant keep going on like that.

ALMOST HOME

We kept arguing with the insurance company about the final check that we were due from the flood insurance company. We called them several times a week, every week. Finally, we were told that it was mailed to us and once we receive it we had to send it to our mortgage company to endorse it and that they would send it back to us in order for us to deposit it. What a ridiculous runaround. It made no sense. It is our house and we are going to use the money to rebuild it. Why does it have to be endorsed by the mortgage company? It took weeks to get done. When we finally received it we sent it to the mortgage company over night with return receipt. We heard from them almost a week later that they had received it and that they were going to have to send an adjuster to the house to make sure that we were actually putting the money into the house before they would release the check. I think that they found a legal loophole that allowed them to take the money, deposit it in their account and make people wait in some cases months before relinquishing the money. That whole time that they had all of that money in their account, it collects interest that they keep. What a racket. Regardless of their indiscretions, they finally sent the adjuster who said that we were doing what we said that we were doing and they sent us the check. It took about a week to get to us. When it was finally deposited we felt much better, like an enormous weight had been lifted off of our shoulders. We could finally afford to start to pay people back who had borrowed money from.

Julie had filled out the paper work for the SBA loan which we were approved for. We were told that if you were approved for the SBA loan that you were ineligible for receiving the FEMA grants. We decided to make the best of a bad situation. We were able to get an appointment with SBA loan personnel and we got an appointment for 2 days later. We signed all of the papers and now all we had to do was wait for them to finish the paper work on their end and send us the check. Eventually, we received a check for about 1/3 of the total amount. They had the audacity to tell us what we could to spend it on and that they would need receipts to prove that we spent it on what they said that we were allowed to. I don't understand why they are allowed to dictate what I spend MY money on. They said that we had to spend it on content. Again, Julie and I decided to make lemonade when life gave us lemons. We decided to get the couch of our dreams that we would have normally never been able to afford. We went to Raymore and Flanagan because they were offering 15% off for Hurricane Sandy victims. We bought a leather sectional sleeper with a recliner and a reclining chaise. We were so excited to get the new couch we could hardly stand it. We decided to give the old material sectional sleeper couch away to someone who was affected by Hurricane Sandy. We gave it to the daughter and son in-law of one of our Rabbis and felt very good about that decision.

At this point Julie and I were going to the house almost every night after the kids went to sleep. We were unpacking boxes and hanging pictures. Finally, Baruch Hashem we got the call that the kitchen installer was going to come and install the kitchen in a few days. The next day the cabinets were delivered and put into the dining room. I couldn't believe how much room they took up. There was barely enough room to squeeze through to get to the kitchen area, but I was happy to be inconvenienced by the boxes that would soon be our kitchen. We continued to unpack our boxes. It was a tedious and painstaking job to unpack them all and reorganize the house. Eventually we finished and it was a beautiful feeling to look around the house and see what appeared to be more of a home. Next, the kitchen cabinet installer came and got to work. He worked quickly and meticulously. It took him just 2 days to finish installing all of the cabinets and he even cleaned up after himself. The next day the guy who was going to fabricate our kitchen counter out of quartz came to measure as well as build a template for the countertop. I was told that it would take about a week and a half for it to be finished and installed.

At last, we were preparing to officially move back to our practically new home. We began to pack up everything that we had at my parents' house. There was so much stuff. It was hard to believe that we had so many things with us. Between clothing, books, toys, seforim, tools, and safes, we had a lot of work ahead of us. We were up very late cleaning up and packing for the two nights leading up to the day that we had decided to head back to our home. The sleep deprivation was all worth it in the end.

HEADING HOME

It was Sunday, February 17; the Sunday before Purim. This was the day that we had been waiting for with baited breath for almost 4 months. One hundred and thirteen days of being refugees from our own home felt like an eternity, yet it seemed to have been over and done with in the blink of an eye when it was all said and done.

I woke up very early and started to load up the cars. They looked like pack mules on an African safari. The roof rack mounted storage bin was completely filled to its maximum capacity of 35 square feet. My back seats were folded flat in order to maximize my cars storage capacity. It was a good thing that I did that because I needed every square inch of room that I could get. I even had the front passenger seat filled with 3 contractor bags of clothing and other various items.

Julie's car had one of the seats from the middle row folded away and two of the three third row seats were folded flat in order to give us the most cargo room possible. I filled her front passenger seat to capacity and then filled in most everywhere else I could, just leaving enough room for D to be able to squeeze into her seat in the third row. We hugged and kissed Bubbs and Papa and thanked them profusely from the bottom of our hearts for all that they had done for us during this trying time in our lives and the fact that they wanted to continue to do more for us. Words fall short when it comes to being able to adequately thank them for all that they gave us between emotional, financial, and physical support. We will never forget the tremendous chesed that we received. There will never be a way to fully show them the *hakaras ha tov* that they deserve.

After doing our best to thank them for everything, we embarked on our trip to again become residents of our beloved home town of Far Rockaway. Julie and I were talking to each other on the phone for most of the trip. The level of excitement and anticipation was completely overwhelming. I could hear the girls in Julie's car singing and squealing with joy. They were talking about how excited they were to be home again and to be able to have play dates with their friends and to sleep in their own beds again. I took a break from the phone call and listened to the Philip Phillips song, Home. I sang along to each and every word. Even though I had heard it at least a few hundred times since the hurricane made us refugees, this time it held new meaning to me. I sang at the top of my lungs: "Hold on to me as we go, as we roll down this unfamiliar road, and although this wave is stringing us along, just know you're not alone, 'cause I'm going to make this place your home. Settle down, it'll all be clear, don't pay no mind to the demons, they fill you with fear, the trouble might drag you down, if you get lost, you can always be found."

We left a house and finally came back to a home. What to do first? Should we unpack or go buy some food because the refrigerator was empty? We decided to disembark and leave everything in the cars and get into the house as fast as we could unbuckle the car seats and get into the house. Each one of us made sure to give the mezuzah a special kiss upon entering the house. The kids must have run around inside the house for at least a half hour before settling down. They were squealing with delight. Just seeing their happiness filled me with an indescribable feeling of joy and finally a feeling of menuchas ha nefesh.

While they were still running around the house rediscovering their own home I went outside and unpacked the cars to make room for all of the food that we were going to have to buy to restock the refrigerator. Because we didn't have a functional kitchen yet, we decided to order Chinese food. I went out to pick it up and brought it home and we enjoyed our first meal back in the house. Then we decided to go to Brachs to restock the house. It was difficult to pry the kids away from the house in order to head to the store to go get the food that we needed. It was as if we had just given them a new toy that they were anticipating receiving for a long time and then taking them away from it. Finally we got them back in the car and headed to Brachs, the local kosher supermarket. We were on cloud nine. We skipped up and down the aisles of Brachs without a care in the world. By the time we were done, we had filled one and a half shopping carts and headed back to our home. By now the sun had already set and it was dark outside. Life felt wonderful again. Nothing could bring us down. We were finally back in our home; going to sleep in our own beds and all seemed to be right with the world, until it wasn't. While we were driving back toward the house and were only about 2 or 3 minutes away from our destination when we noticed a gigantic flash of light on the horizon that lit up the large apartment building that was behind it. The flash of light was immediately followed by the sound of an explosion. I asked Julie if she had seen what I thought that I saw. She confirmed that it wasn't just my imagination and we began to worry. The location of the explosion and flash of light was only about two blocks away from our home. I started to drive quickly. My mind was at the mercy of my imagination. Horrible scenarios began to swirl around inside my head. I remember saying to Julie, "not again, I can't handle anything else". I could see the fear on her face, it was as plain as day. When we got to the Nassau Expressway everything seemed to be fine. There were no fires, no sirens, no smell of smoke, and the streetlights and houses had their lights on. As we drew closer to the house and got off at the Segirt Blvd exit we realized what had happened. All of the street lights were out. All of the houses had no lights on. I thought to myself, "not again, not another blackout". We kept driving toward the house and Julie tried to be an optimist while I had sunken into a murky pessimistic mood. She said "maybe it is just over here; maybe we will have power at our house". I asked her if we should call my parents and ask them if we could spend one more night at their house again. Luckily Julie was being rational and positive enough for the both of us. She said that maybe it's just temporary and the power will come back in a few minutes. While we were driving down our block I realized that we had 10 gallons of gas in gas cans in the shed but we didn't have a generator anymore. I also realized that we needed a generator because I needed to power the sub-pump in the French drain in order to prevent the basement from flooding again. And what were we going to do with all of the food that we had just bought that

required refrigeration? I realized that the explosion was from a power trans-
former on a telephone pole had exploded. I told Julie that I had to get to
Lowe's as quickly as I could. She told me to pull into the driveway and to get
into my car and head to Lowe's. Baruch Hashem my ayshes chiyil (woman of
valor) said that she would unpack the food in the car and bring the kids into
the house. I was In panic mode and don't remember if I said thank you or not
but I ran into the house and got my keys, setup and turned on a few flashlights so they would be able to see and I headed out to Lowe's to get a new
generator. I have made that same Lowe's trip countless times before, never
driving this quickly though. In my head I kept thinking that my car was rac-
ing against the water level in the French drain. I was hoping that I would be
able to get to Lowe's, buy a generator, bring it back home, set it up, and get it
started before the basement started to flood. About 2 or 3 minutes later
while I was driving like a maniac towards Lowe's I received a phone call from
Julie. As soon as I answered the call I heard Julie enthusiastically say "Baruch
Hashem the power came back on and everything's working". I took a deep
breath and started to relax again and drive like a normal human being. I was
so happy that we didn't have to leave the house again. Julie said that I should
just turn around and come home. I told her that I was still going to go to
Lowe's and buy a new generator because it was still a necessity to have in our
home. I explained that with all of the repairs that were going on to the electrical system in our neighborhood because of the hurricane we might still
have blackouts from time to time. I also mentioned that our neighbors who
were able to move back onto our block about 2 months earlier than us had
told us that blackouts had become commonplace but in general they were
short lived. I further explained that if the power goes out and it is raining
outside that we would only have 2 or 3 minutes to turn on the generator before the 33 gallon drum of the French drain would start to overflow and we
would have a flooded basement again. Julie agreed with me and I continued
on my way to Lowe's. By this point, my nerves were shot, I quickly went to
the section with generators, which by this time they had an excess of and
picked out a new generator. This time I wasn't forced to buy the only model
that they had. I used my cellphone to go online and check Consumer Re-
ports to see what they had to say about each model. I didn't want to buy one

that was expensive and then have it die after only 10.5 hours of use again. I chose a smaller model than the one that I had previously purchased because the older larger one that I had had was overkill for what I needed. I chose one that was strong enough to do what I needed it to do and light enough that I would be able to schlep it up the stairs and outside by myself relatively quickly. I loaded it in the trunk and headed home once again. I left the generator in my trunk and went inside the house. It was already bed time for the kids. We had a big surprise in store for our youngest daughter, Miriam. When we had left our house because of the hurricane she was still sleeping her crib. We had already gotten her a twin sized bed that was given to us by Julie's great aunt Rita. We just didn't switch her to the bed yet for some reason. While at my parents' house she slept in a junior bed and was fine with it. When we brought her to her room she just stopped walking once she stepped into her room and saw the bed. The bed had pink sheets, and a pink comforter with a butterfly pattern all over it. She looked up at us and asked us who was going to be sleeping in her room instead of her. Julie and I looked at each other and smiled. Julie knelt down beside Miriam and told her that she was a big girl now and that it was her bed. Miriam's eyes grew wide and just when her smile seemed to take over her face she leapt onto Julies legs and wrapped her arms around her and gave her a huge hug and buried her face into Julie's neck and said "tank you mommy". The scene was priceless. I wish that I had a camera on me. Once the girls were asleep we spent about an hour putting things away, organizing, and cleaning. We decided that with all that had happened that day, we deserved to go to sleep early. I must say, as comfortable as the beds were at Bubbe and Papas' house, my bed felt like heaven. Knowing that I was finally home and about to sleep in my own bed was the cherry on top of the coming home sundae. Even the girls went to sleep more easily in their own beds. Julie reminded me that I could set my alarm to wake me up later because we were home again and our house is closer to Coney than my parents' house. Julie and I had a celebratory lechiam and went to sleep. I woke up in the morning refreshed and well rested. It felt wonderful to wake up in my own bed, in our bed room, in our own home, in our neighborhood that we love so much. I was so happy that I remember singing while brushing my teeth and brushing my hair. I listened to the Philip Phillips song for the entire drive to work. I was filled with such an overwhelming feeling of being bisimcha that when I got to work everyone noticed a difference. I was told that I was constantly smiling and had an extra spring in my step. Whenever anyone would ask me what had happened that made me so happy, I gladly told them that Baruch Hashem we had just moved back into our home and that I couldn't be happier.

Later that night we were deciding what to do for dinner. We still didn't have a finished kitchen so cooking was out of the question. We became sidetracked with something else and said that we would talk about it later on. Just then we received a phone call from our partner. She was telling us that she was in Manhattan at a function and that she was going to take home the left overs. She asked us if we were interested in the leftovers for dinner. She warned us that there was a lot of food. We said yes please and thanked her again. When she came to the house we saw what a lot of food was. There were four trays of food. Each tray was 4 inches deep and at least 2 feet wide. There was rice, vegetables, meat, chicken, salad, potatoes, and more. Nothing was from a simple recipe. Everything was prepared in an extravagant manner. We were truly eating like kings. We ended up eating from those trays for several days. We couldn't believe that we were already living back at our house and she was still constantly calling and texting and e-mailing us with opportunities to receive help and with things that people wanted to donate to us. What a magnificent mench.

The next day we received a letter in the mail from the Red Cross. We were waiting to hear from them about the grant so I just stared at the letter for a little while before opening it. I was excited and nervous at the same time. When I finally had the courage to open it I saw that it said that we were in the final stages of being approved. We had to send them some paperwork and that we would receive another phone call from them shortly to schedule an interview in our home. A few days later we received the phone call from the Red Cross that we were waiting for and we set an appointment for the interview for the beginning of the next week. On Tuesday of the next week we had our interview with them and they asked for a tour of our home and property to see what damage was done and what repairs were made. They asked us about how much it cost to make the repairs and how much we had received from our insurance company. After that they told us that they would be in touch with us about what the determination was about how much if any money we could expect in the form of a grant.

2 or 3 days later we got a call from the kitchen counter top installer. He said that it was ready and that we would be able to come the next day to install the countertops. We were so excited to have a finished kitchen that was so much better, more beautiful, and larger than the kitchen that we had before the hurricane. When he came the next day he only needed about a half hour to install the countertops, sinks, and to drill the holes in the countertop for the faucets and soap dispensers. The next day we had the cabinet installer come back to hook up the plumbing for the faucets and install the faucets. We finally had a finished and functional kitchen and it was absolutely beautiful.

Our new kitchen that was a dramatic improvement from the old one

It was a few days before Purim and we still didn't know what we were going to dress up as. The previous year we all made our own costumes. We were all monsters. We didn't have enough time to make a new costume. We didn't know what to do. Julie decided to check out the Purim costume gemachs to see what they still had. She and the girls decided that they were going to dress up as princesses and that I should dress up as a prince. I decided to dress up as the king instead. I got a kings crown and I decided to buy a pair of Elvis Presley sunglasses and then I was going to trim my beard very short except for leaving the Elvis sideburns. That way I would be the king in 2 ways. My wonderful wife decided that that wasn't enough. She decided that I needed something else; something to make me stand out in a crowd. When she brought it home to show me she told me that I had to agree to wear it before I saw it. My girls had already seen it and said that they loved it and that I have to wear it because it was so funny. Reluctantly, I agreed because Julie and the girls have been through so much, I just wanted to make them happy. When they showed it to me my jaw dropped. It was a horse costume that I put on like suspenders that made me look like I was riding the horse. When we were walking around the neighborhood, it looked like a king riding on his horse surrounded by 4 princesses.

Our family purim picture while we deliver shalochmanos

At first it was embarrassing but after a while of seeing Julie and the girls laughing out loud and smiling I was fine with it because if they are happy then I am happy. We did our usual Purim day schedule. After davening we got dressed up and gave out the shalochmanos to the neighbors that are on our block and then we got into the car and went to Kew Gardens to go and give shalochmanos to a very special family; the Greenbergs. The Greenberg family has had more hashpa'ah on this world litov than just about anyone else. Rabbi and Rebetzin Jeffrey Greenberg are the reason why my mother is frum, my sister and her children are frum and why Julie and I and our children are frum today. I hope that Rebetzin Greenberg will me mochel me for calling her Rebetzin in the book. She doesn't even like to be called Mrs. Greenberg. She introduced herself as Naomi and if you call her Rebetzin or Mrs. Greenberg she will ignore you if you are one of their NCSYers. The Greenberg family is definitely counted amongst the lamed vuv hidden tzadeekim in this world. Rabbi Greenberg used to be the head of the New York City region of NCSY and the director of NCSYs' kiruv camp in Baltimore, Camp Sports. He has made hundreds if not thousands of people frum who in turn have most likely caused tens of thousands of people to be frum from birth if not more. My families' relationship with Rabbi and Rebetzin Greenberg Goes back almost 20 years but my families' relationship with NCSY goes back much further than that. My Tanta Mindy was the first person in our family to become frum as a teenager and it was brought about through NCSY. While my family was not religious we were very Jewishly oriented. Tanta Mindy always did her best to infuse our lives with yiddishkite where ever and whenever possible. When she found out that NCSY was going to be starting a chapter of their Jr. NCSY in the conservative synagogue that we attended she was instrumental in having my sister who is 4 years older than me go. Because we were always enrolled in New York City public schools this would be a nice way to meet other Jewish children. We would play sports and eat pizza and have shabbatons. These are weekends with lots of other Jewish teenagers with some NCSY staff where we went to hotels or people's houses and had programs with activities and classes that taught us about various parts of yiddishkite. Once we got to ninth grade we went to Sr. NCSY which is where we met Rabbi and Rebetzin Greenberg. Eventually my sister became frum and then my mother became frum and eventually I became frum. My father did not become frum, but Rabbi Greenberg always made sure that while I was caught up in the enthusiasm of becoming frum to make sure that I always was respectful toward my father. He alwayse told me not look down upon him because he was allowing me to do what I wanted to and to change my life in a way that he didn't necessarily agree with. For that and thousands of other reasons, we go to Queens to deliver only 1 shalochmonos. When we got to his house Rabbi Greenberg wasn't there but everyone else was. Julie was met by Rebetzin Greenberg with a big hug. We have known their children ever since they were very young. We schmoozed with them for a while while their kids played with ours. We thought that it was a beautiful thing, practically a dream come true that our children are playing with Rabbi and Rebetzin Greenberg's kids. Once Rabbi Greenberg came home I got a big hug and we all schmoozed for a while. They asked us how we were doing and how things were going. I don't think that they expected to hear about as much happening as we exposed them to. We told them all about what we had gone through, continue to go through, and what else we have to go through. After staying at their house for around a half hour we left and went back to Far Rockaway to finish delivering our shalochmonos to our friends and Rebeim. Once we were done with our deliveries we went to our partners' house for our Purim seuda. It was a beautiful and leibadik seuda. After finishing our Purim seuda it was time to go back to our house because it was already past the girls' bed time.

Finally the day came when we got the phone call from the Red Cross telling us that we were going to be receiving a $10,000 grant. We were overjoyed because we were going to, Baruch Hashem, be receiving more help. We decided that the money was going to go towards paying for the French drain in the new room as well as replacing all of our windows. Some of our windows leaked before the hurricane. After the hurricane the windows that leaked a little bit leaked a lot more and the windows that didn't lead were leaking now. We didn't want the old windows to continue to leak and ruin all of the work that had been done on the first floor or the basement. I made a few phone calls and found out if there is a reputable window guy to call in Far Rockaway. I kept getting the same name. His name is Mordachie Weinreb. We called him to come to the house and give us an estimate. When he came to the house he measured the windows and he gave us an estimate that was more than fair. The $10,000 grant would almost be enough to cover the French drain and the windows, Baruch Hashem. Seeyata deshmaya is truly a beautiful thing. About a week and a half later he came in installed all of the 16 windows in just 2 days and did a beautiful job with both the installation and the cleaning up after himself.

About two weeks before Pesach I realized that we were going to be going away to Atlanta Georgia to spend Pesach with my sister and her family and that our house had no alarm system installed. I felt uncomfortable leaving our house unprotected for that long. Again I made a few phone calls to find out who was a good alarm installer to use because I didn't want to use the old alarm company that we had previously, because they were unreliable. I heard about a guy named Zev Cohen who had a very good reputation for being reliable as well as doing good work. I called him and he came to give us an estimate. He told us that he wouldn't have time before Pesach to install the entire alarm but he would send his installer to install the main system, keypads, smoke detectors, motion sensor, and alarm the doors. That way the house would be protected until after Pesach when he would be available to come and install the rest of the alarm.

We had decided that it was time to make another kiddush. This time, in our home, for our community. We sent out a text message invitations as well as called people to invite them and told them that we were making a kiddush in our home to show our *hakaras ha tov* to the Reboneh Shel Olum and to our friends who helped us get through that difficult period of time In our lives. We decided to order some of the food as well as have Julie do some of the cooking. We had chulent, potato kugel, cakes, cookies, liquor, and much more. It was the Shabbos of March 16th. It was a beautiful day outside and even more beautiful inside our home. We must have had at least 80 to 90 people that came and went throughout the two hour kiddush. It really made us feel welcomed home by our friends, neighbors, and community. We haven't decided yet for sure, but we might start to make an annual kiddush on the anniversary of us moving back into the house.

Finally it was time to go to my sisters' house in Atlanta for Pesach with the menuchas hanefesh of knowing that the alarm was installed and the house was almost completely finished. We had a beautiful Pesach with my sister and brother-in-law and their kids and Bubbe and Papa and their dog Charlie. Everywhere we went people heard we were from Far Rockaway and ask how we were affected by the hurricane. Every time we told people what we went through and about the chesed, nisim, and seeyatadeshmaya that we were zocheh to receive, everyone said that I should write a book about it. They all said that it would bring people chizuk, emuna, and betachon. They also said that outside of our neighborhood no one knew about what was going on as far as the community rising to the challenge. Finally their relentless calls for me to write a book lit a fire under me to get started on my writing journey. As soon as we came back to Far Rockaway after Pesach, even though our story hadn't yet finished, I started to write while the rest of our story continued to unfold.

A week after Pesach our entire alarm system was installed. I was able to sleep soundly knowing that we were safe and secure in our practically brand new home. Every once in a while we would have Sandy flashbacks which caused us to appreciate everything that we had gone through and what we now have.

When the girls returned to school we were made aware of something called Project Hope. Project Hope was an organization that would help children who were affected by Hurricane Sandy to cope with what they had gone through and minimize the psychological aftermath. They had story telling groups with the children where they would share their experiences with each other and be able to see that they were not alone. They also offered free therapy for children who were not able to cope with the losses that they had suffered. When Basya and Devora Nechama would come home they would tell us about the story telling and arts and crafts groups that Project Hope was having them participate in. It was truly a beautiful thing to see the community coming together again to help Sandy's youngest victims. Towards the end of the school year Devora Nechama was told to write her own book about whatever she wanted. She chose to write about our experiences before, during and after Hurricane Sandy and titled it, "Believe in Rebonoh Shel Olam". It was a fantastic book about the positive aspects of chesed and Divine protection that we lived through.

Several weeks later we received a phone call from our partner. This time she was telling us that there was going to be a special program where people who had lost their bicycles to Sandy would be given new bikes. We told her how many bikes we had lost and their sizes and we were told that they would get in touch with us when it was time to pick them up. We were elated at the news that we would be getting new bikes. My girls were tingling with anticipation. They asked us practically every day if the next day was the day that they were going to be getting them. It didn't matter how many times we told them that it wouldn't be for a few weeks, they kept on asking and asking and asking. Finally, bicycle day had come. I made 2 trips to the bicycle store to pick up the bikes and bring them back home while the kids were eating dinner. The looks on their faces were priceless when they saw 5 shiny new bikes in the backyard, some with multicolored tassels and some with baskets. They were so excited that they had to sit on the bikes with their helmets and try them out.

The girls with their new bicycles that were donated to us

About a month or so after we had returned home after Pesach I had heard people talking about a neighborhood watch called the RCSP. The Rockaway Citizen Safety Patrol is the Far Rockaway/Bayswater chapter of Shomrim. It is comprised of a group of volunteers that do more for the community than anyone knows. Its members patrol our neighborhoods while its residents are sleeping. Its members offer assistance wherever, whenever, and however, possible. Its members canvas our streets looking for missing persons, stolen property, and fugitives from the law. Its members locate and process video footage from crime scenes and hand it over to the police in order for them to make numerous arrests. Its members put themselves into harm's way while the general public in our neighborhood are unaware of their existence. They are among Far Rockaways unsung heroes. I was told that they were patrolling the neighborhood after Hurricane Sandy to not only avoid the looting of houses, but also to make people feel safer in their houses knowing that there were vigilant tzadikim out there doing their best to keep them safe and out of harm's way. They patrolled during the day and throughout the night selflessly without asking for any recognition in return. I was told that during and throughout the immediate and extended aftermath of Hurricane Sandy, with the help from the surrounding areas' Shomrim chapters they had at least 6 cars patrolling the area 24 hours a day, 6 days a week. They also had people patrolling on foot on Shabbos. I was also told that the 101st Precinct increased their patrols in our neighborhoods on Shabbos because Shomrim was unable to patrol with cars and radios. Shomrim supplied and maintained generators, pumped the water out of peoples basements, gave food and support to the sick and infirmed, cordoned off flooded and unsafe areas, took part in searches for missing persons, had a manned hotline 24 hour a day, went in to shuls of our area and the surrounding areas to safeguard both damaged and undamaged Sifrei Torah and seforim, and saved people from flooded areas and cars. The surrounding areas of Far Rockaway and Bayswater that were outside of the Jewish area saw a seven fold rise in crime from what it was previously. Thanks to the Shomrim patrols, the rise in crime in the Jewish area was minute. Several months after the fact, I found out that some of the tzadeekim that helped me to empty my basement and pack up and move our remaining belongings were members of Shomrim (RCSP). For protecting my home from being looted, keeping my community safe, and for doing so much more, I will always be grateful. Since then I have joined Shomrim as unit 51 and hope to continue to be an active member as long as the need exists.

Unfortunately we were still in financial need. We still owed more than twenty thousand dollars to family members and the contractor. Once again

I was told to talk to Yitzie Halpern because he was involved in making sure that money that was earmarked from chesed organizations made its way to those in need. He was able to procure ten thousand dollars from the Community Assistance Fund and another ten thousand dollars an organization called Chasdei Yisroel. The only words that come to mind while I am typing this are nisim vi'niflaos. The chesed of Jews really knows no bounds. Baruch Hashem, that allowed us to pay off the overwhelming majority of our debt.

At this point I was on a first name basis with our case manager from the Red Cross. I had been calling her almost every day making sure that she had all of the correct information and making sure to be a thorn in her side until we received our needed grant money. I was being overly persistent because not only did we need the money, but I had read that the Red Cross was starting to deny most of the people who were originally approved for the grant for no apparent reason and hiding behind red tape. For over a month I was told on a regular basis that we would have it by the end of the week or that the check was in the mail. During that final month of waiting for the check, our contractor came back into the picture. We had to have the cement staircase near the main entrance of the house demolished and replaced. It had suffered severe damage during the Hurricane and was continuing to deteriorate. We told Barry that we didn't have all of the money in our hands but that we should be getting the money from the Red Cross grant "any day now" and would give him half of the money upfront and the rest when we had it. After all, we were told that we would receive the check at any moment and we trusted them for some reason. Originally we were going to have them rebuild the staircase out of decking material to the same specifications as the previous staircase which would allow it to be hollow. This would leave us a space to put our garbage cans underneath and we would be able to put another window under the staircase for increased ventilation in the basement. After much deliberation we decided to continue the landing at the top of the staircase and have it continue along the entire side of the house and attach it to our deck in the backyard which would add another 4 feet to the width of our existing deck. We then decided that we should replace the awning that we had above the staircase because it was damaged but this time to have Barry make it out of wood and clear plastic and to have it run the length of the side of the house. What a moment of seyata deshmaya that was. We were told that it would cost us an additional sixteen hundred to two thousand dollars to have the rubble from the demolished staircase removed and that it would probably be closer to the higher end of the spectrum. We didn't know where the money was going to come from. Bichasdei Hashem, the night before I was supposed to finalize with my contractor that his rubble remover was to get the job I was throwing out some garbage outside the house and a white van happened to be driving by. We looked at each other and he rolled down his window and asked me if I was looking for someone to haul away all of the rubble. I told him that I already had someone that was going to do it and he got out of his van and said that he would be able to beat their price by a significant amount. He ended up doing it for us for twelve hundred dollars and he took a significant amount of other debris and garbage that was lying around in the back and side yard. Between the demolition and rebuilding of the staircase, the walkway and awning on the side of the house, the deck extension, the new window in the basement, and some odds and ends inside the house came out to an astronomical ten thousand dollars that we didn't have. Barry was a real mensch about it. He asked us to give him what we could and to call him to pick up the rest when we could spare it. When it was finished it was absolutely beautiful. It changed the essence of the entire house. It is an outside room that faces the wetlands and makes you feel like you are up in the country.

A picture of the house about a month after the hurricane

A picture of what the house looks like now

MAKEH VI POTISH

lmost a month went by and finally the day came when I opened the mailbox and found the envelope from the Red Cross. Our check had finally come. I called Barry to tell him that the check had arrived and that we could now finish paying him even before I called Julie. A few days later Barry came to the house and we were finally able to finish paying for all of the construction that it took to rebuild our home. It was a surreal experience handing him that check and not owing anyone money anymore. To top it all off, later that week I received a four hundred dollar gift card from the company that I work for because I was a Sandy victim.

Several months later we were again contacted by our partner who went on to tell us that Leiters sukkah company was going to be offering substantial discounts for the purchase of new sukkahs for Hurricane Sandy victims who had either lost their sukkahs or whose sukkahs were damaged in the storm. Since we were able to extend our deck we were able to go from an 8X12 sukkah to a 10X16 and paid less than we would have for the 8X12. I found out that both Leiters and the local distributer each lowered their profit margin on these sukkahs which when combined came out to a 25% discount which made a big difference.

At some point in February we had received an email from our partner about a governmental program for assisting Hurricane Sandy victims financially with a grant. The organization is called Build It Back. Julie immediately went online and registered with them and they said that we should hear back from them in the "near future". We were contacted by them in July and we were told about a mountain of prepared documents that we would need to show proof of loss and proof of what we had received from insurance. Baruch Hashem Julie is so incredibly organized. Julie had everything that we needed nicely organized in an accordion organizer that Papa had provided us for just such an occasion. On a Sunday morning we went to Fort Tilden in Breezy Point to meet with them and go through the motions of explaining what had happened and showing them all of the paper work so that they can input it into their database to see if we were eligible for further grants. According to them, we should be qualified for their grant but the actual amount was not yet determined. We are still awaiting their call for when they would like to come and do a home inspection for further review of our case. Im'yirtza Hashem things will go well in the right time. While we were speaking to the staff of the Build It Back program we had mentioned how we were denied FEMA assistance within the first week post Hurricane Sandy, and that we were told that because we were above the poverty line we were ineligible for the grant. The Build It Back staff member was outraged at what we were telling her. She told us that there is no income restriction with being approved for a FEMA grant. She told us that we were lied to and that we should reapply for FEMA and get a lawyer if we have to because we were neglected and given false information about our situation. We are still on the fence about reapplying because we personally know people who also sustained damage from the hurricane and were denied FEMA assistance who have reapplied several times and been summarily denied repeatedly.

What a year this has been. I would have never dreamed that my family and I would have been put through the laundry list of trials and tribulations that we can now talk about in past tense. It has truly been filled with eye opening experiences, each one greater than the last. We have found strength through the Rebonoh Shel Olam, our friends, our family, our community, and from Klal Yisroel as a whole. As alone as we may have felt from time to time, the truth couldn't have been farther from the reality. In hindsight, for the last 10 months there was only one set of footprints, we were never alone, we were being carried. It has truly been an amazing opportunity for so many people to take part in chesed on such an unprecedented level, to come together to help so many people in need. We didn't know how we were going to financially and spiritually get through it all. We would never have imagined that when our insurance gave us about half of what we needed that the other half would be sent to us from the Rebonoh Shel Olam through his holy people, both private individuals and chesed organizations. When our emuna was shaken, He sent us our Rabbeim, friends, and family to lift us up. Each time that He sent us help, we couldn't imagine that there would be more to come and yet there always was. I wish that I could thank everyone who helped us, but I would need to make a second volume of the book to do it justice. This experience has truly shown me the greatness of the yiddishe neshama. So many people worked day and night behind the scenes to do so much for so many that they didn't even know. To all of Hashem's tzadikim, both known to me and who were behind the scenes, I thank you from the bottom of my heart.

If He would have just saved us from the tidal surge and destructive winds of the Hurricane, it would have been enough.

If He would have just given us half of the money that we needed to rebuild and not sent us to Achiezer, Nivneh, the Community Assistance Fund, or Chasdei Yisroel, it would have been enough.

If He would have just let us move back into our house without sending us our partner who did so much chesed on our behalf, it would have been enough.

If He would have just saved us from dangers that were obvious, that would have been enough.

If He would have just saved us from dangers that were hidden, it would have been enough.

But, for Him, it wasn't. He saw fit to make us whole again physically, spiritually, emotionally, and financially. For all that the Rebonoh Shel Olam has done and continues to do for us; I thank Hashem from the depths of my being.

AFTERWORD

I originally started to write this book as a reminder of what we went through and as an enduring record of the *nisim* that we witnessed and the *chesed* that we received for future generations. I didn't want to forget even the smallest aspect of our tumultuous journey, not the highest of highs and not the lowest of lows.

If it had not been for these fantastic *chesed* organizations we would have had a very different story to tell. It would have been only lows without their reciprocal highs. Rav Dovid Goldwasser said, in a *sefer* called *Step by Step,* that in *birchos hashachar* we have the blessing *baruch ata Hashem....... pokei'ach ivrim,* which means that Hashem should open up our eyes so that we are able to see the *hashgacha* in our lives. Hurricane Sandy caused our lows; these *chesed* organizations caused our highs, which made it possible for us to be able to see the world according to Rav Dovid Goldwasser's interpretation of the blessing of *pokei'ach ivrim.*

During the process of writing everything down in book form I realized that it could be so much more than a keepsake. I came to realize that not only could it be used for posterity's sake but it could be used as a tool to show my *hakaras ha tov* to all of the wonderful *chesed* organizations whose selfless work was not only appreciated but was so vital to so many people in order for them to rebuild their lives, my own included. I am asking all of the people who have decided to buy and read this book to please help them continue their selfless work. I am urging you to please find it in your hearts to donate what you can to them and to make them permanent fixtures in your *cheshbon* of charities that you donate *tzedakah* to. Without the previous donations, these *tzadikim* would not have been able to undertake and succeed in their herculean task of helping so many members of *Klal Yisroel*. Please help them to be able to continue to help so many people who are in need. The amount of *chesed* that they are able to do is directly affected by the donations that they receive. As unbelievable as the amount of *chesed* that my family and I received, it is just a drop in the bucket when compared to all of the other families that they have affected by their selfless deeds. I cannot stress enough how important it is to support them. They deserve your help. It is my hope that you should never need their help but I know that if anyone is ever in need of their assistance that they will always be there to help. I believe that they are truly helping to bring Moshiach speedily in our days.

ORGANIZATIONS

In order to be able to donate to these wonderful organizations their contact information is listed below:

Nivneh
www.nivneh.org

1(516)508-9997

Checks can be made out to "Nivneh" and mailed to 1056 New McNeil Ave, Lawrence, NY, 11559

The Davis Memorial Fund (CAF)
www.Davismemorialfund.org

1(866)587-8448

Checks can be made out to "Davis Memorial Fund INC" and mailed to 25 Lawrence Avenue, Lawrence, NY, 11559

Achiezer
www.Achiezer.org

1(516)791-4444

Checks can be made out to "Achiezer" and mailed to 334 Central Avenue, Lawrence, NY, 11559

The JCCRP
www.JCCRP.org

1(718)327-7755

Checks can be made out to "JCCRP" and mailed to 1525 Central Avenue, Far Rockaway, NY, 11691

The MET Council
www.metcouncil.org

1(212)453-9649

Checks can be made out to "Met council" and mailed to 120 Broadway, 7th floor, NY, 10271

The Rockaway Citizens Safety Patrol (Shomrim)
www.fidelipay.com/RCSP

Checks can be made out to "Rockaway Citizen's Safety Patrol" and mailed to C/O A. Frankel 774 Caffrey Avenue, Far Rockaway, NY, 11691

Yeshiva Sh'or Yoshuv
www.shoryoshuv.org

Checks can be made out to "Sh'or Yoshuv Institute" and mailed to 1 Cedar Lawn Avenue, Lawrence, NY, 11559

Three times a day, every day, I am reminded of what Hashem did for us and for people like us when I say "*Aleinu l'shabei'ach laAdon Hakol*" we thank and praise Hashem for all the *chassadim* he has done for us using these *chesed* organizations as his tools within his *teva*. Please assist them in their herculean efforts to continue to help *Klal Yisroel*. Thank you for reading our story.